A
CULTURAL HISTORY
OF POSTWAR JAPAN
1945-1980

A
CULTURAL HISTORY
OF POSTWAR JAPAN
1945-1980
Shunsuke Tsurumi

Routledge
Taylor & Francis Group

LONDON AND NEW YORK

First published in Japanese in 1984 by Iwanami Shoten, Tokyo
This edition published in 1987, reprinted 1990, 1994 by
Kegan Paul International Limited

This edition first published in 2009
by Routledge
2 Park Square, Milton Park, Abingdon, Oxon, OX14 4RN
711 Third Avenue, New York, NY 10017

Routledge is an imprint of the Taylor & Francis Group, an informa business

First issued in paperback 2016

© This translation kegan Paul International Limited 1987

Transferred to Digital Printing 2009

British Library Cataloguing in Publication Data
A catalogue record for this book is available from the British Library

ISBN13: 978-0-7103-0259-5 (hbk)
ISBN13: 978-1-138-96708-3 (pbk)

Publisher's Note
The publisher has gone to great lengths to ensure the quality of this reprint
but points out that some imperfections in the original copies may be
apparent. The publisher has made every effort to contact original copyright
holders and would welcome correspondence from those they have been
unable to trace.

Contents

Acknowledgements

Photograph 1 *Mainichi Shinbun.* Photographed by Kimura
Ihei (in *Asahi Kamera*, Special Issue, December
1979).
2 *Asahi Shinbun*
3–4 *Mainichi Shinbun*
5 Photographed by Kimura Ihei (*Machikado –
Street Scenes* – Nikon Saron Bukkusu, Vol. 7)
6 Shirato Sanpei, *Ninja Bugeichō*, Vol. 16-B,
Kagemaruden (The Life of Kagemaru),
Shōgakkan, 1971, p. 108
7 Mizuki Shigeru, *Kappa no Sanpei* (Sanpei the
Kappa), Vol. 4, Asahi Sonorama, 1970, p. 220
8 Tsuge Yoshiharu, *Tsuge Yoshiharu-shū* (Selected
Works of Tsuge Yoshiharu), *Gendai Manga*,
Vol. 12, Chikuma Shobō, 1970, p. 247
9 Takemiya Keiko, *Tera e . . .* (Earthward
bound . . .), Monthly *Manga Shōnen*, Special
Issue, General edition, Part I, Asahi Sonorama,
1977, p. 110
10 Yamagami Tatsuhiko, *Gaki Deka*, Vol. II,
Shōnen Chanpion Komikkusu, Akita Shoten,
1975, p. 144
12 Ishiguro Keishichi, *Utsusareta Bakumatsu* (The
Bakumatsu Period in Photos), Vol. II, Asoka
Shobō, 1957, p. 45
13 *Suikyō Kijinden* (Lives of Whimsical Eccentrics),
1863, Sandaibanashi Kaijō. By courtesy of
Mr Tachibana Ukon
14 *Shinsakubanashi Omoshiro Sugoroku*, 1883. By
courtesy of Mr Tachibana Ukon

12, 16, 17, 18   By courtesy of Magajin *Haususha*
20   Photographed by Kimura Tsunehisa. First appeared in *Kikan Shashin Eizō*, No. 3, 1969
19, 21–27   Courtesy of NHK Service Centre
28–29   By courtesy of Suntory
31   Photograph of Kimura Ihei. From *Kimura Ihei no Me*, Special Issue of *Asahi Kamera*, 1970
32   Courtesy of Maruhachi Mawata
33–34   Courtesy of Magajin *Haususha*

Score   3   *Peppā Keibu* 1976 by N.T.V.N.M. & Nichion Inc.
4   *Haru Ichiban* (The First Storm of Spring), 1976 by Watanabe Music Publishing Corporation.

Photograph 35   Courtesy of Tōhō
Score   14   *Kaette Kita Yopparai* (The drunk who came back), 1967, by ART Music Publishing Co., Ltd.
Photograph 39–40   Courtesy of Asahi Shinbunsha
37–38   Hasegawa Machiko, *Sazaesan*, Vol. 46, Shimaisha, 1969, p. 68
41   Courtesy of Mainichi Shinbunsha
42   Sophy Hoare, *Japan, the land and its people*, in *Macdonald Countries* series, Macdonald Educational, London, 1975, p. 36
43   *Lat's Lot* (second collection), Berita Publishing Sdn. Bhd., Kuala Lumpur, 1978, p. 126.

List of Illustrations

To Charles W. Young

Preface

Japan's surrender on 15 August 1945 was an unprecedented event in Japanese history. The shift from the life of hunger to the life of saturation that took place between 1945 and 1980 has brought about a great change in life style. The significance of this change will be a subject of reassessment for many years to come. Here I have tried to present an outline of such a change in the domain of mass culture, a sector of Japanese culture most indicative of the change after the defeat and the subsequent economic recovery.

This book, like the earlier one, *An Intellectual History of Wartime Japan, 1931–1945*, is based on a series of lectures I gave at McGill University, Quebec, Canada. The lectures were delivered in English from 17 January to 20 March 1980. The footnotes were prepared for the Japanese version published by Iwanami Shoten in 1984.

I am grateful to the East Asia Centre, McGill University, and the Japan Foundation. My thanks are due to Professors Paul Lin, Sam Noumoff, Ward Geddes, and Yuzo Ohta, my colleagues at McGill University. Thanks are also due to Ms Alison Tokita of Monash University for her assistance in the preparation of the English text, to Mr Kōji Takamura for the compilation of illustrations which I had not been able to make use of in the lectures, to Professor Norihiro Katō, formerly of the University of Montreal, for generously letting me make use of his record of my lectures in mimeographed form, and to Dr Yoshio Sugimoto of La Trobe University for giving me the opportunity to write this book as well as the earlier one.

This book is dedicated to Mr Charles W. Young, my classmate at Middlesex School, Concord, Massachusetts, U.S.A., in 1938–1939, in recognition of our friendship, which has survived the war between the two nations.

Shunsuke Tsurumi
October 1986
Kyoto

1 Occupation: the American Way of Life as an Imposed Model

On 30 August 1945, the Commander-in-Chief of the Allied Military Forces, General MacArthur, arrived in Japan full of the confidence which characterized his whole life. From air photos taken in the last phase of the war, he was assured that there was little possibility of meeting significant resistance from the Japanese. This made him magnanimous.

General MacArthur had been known as a man of conservative political views. In the summer of 1932, on the order of President Hoover, General MacArthur commanded cavalry and infantry to disperse the 5,000 squatters who remained in barracks in Washington after the spring march of the bonus army, the unemployed World War I veterans who had been badly hit by the 1929 panic. Some 11,000 had marched to Washington to demand the earlier payment of their pension. President Hoover had obtained $100,000 from Congress and reduced the bonus army to 5,000, who then built barracks and continued to watch the central government. The crushing of the remaining bonus army made MacArthur famous. This was just before Hoover was replaced by Roosevelt, who introduced the New Deal. Ironically, at the time of his arrival in Japan General MacArthur's staff officers were men who had grown up in the era of the New Deal. Nevertheless, MacArthur had soldierly affection for these staff officers, who had fought with him in the Philippines and beyond, and was ready to enjoy the task of drawing up a blueprint for the remodelling of Japan in a spirit of magnanimity. In this respect, the background of his subordinate officers – the New Deal era, when the United States government planned the economy and life style of the society – was most helpful.

Subordinate again to these officers were non-commissioned officers just a few years out of university. These did most of the chores of investigating conditions in postwar Japan, an extremely difficult task because cities were burnt down and records removed to faraway country towns, and the personal network which could have supplied needed information was hard to find. The task of gathering information and of applying the directives to concrete cases was often left to these young and energetic non-commissioned officers. The Supreme Commander and his higher-ranking aides did not have time to examine the decisions of subordinates in detail, and in many cases supported subordinates' decisions in the face of complaints brought to them by high-ranking officials of the Japanese government, politicians and company presidents, who had enjoyed a high prestige before the surrender. This state of affairs continued roughly until the outbreak of the Korean War in June 1950, which brought about a change in the atmosphere which had influenced MacArthur's decisions.

So we might say that there was a time-lag between the U.S.A. and U.S. occupied Japan. The earlier phase of the U.S. occupation of Japan perpetuated the original spirit of the New Deal as it had existed in the United States during the early period of the Roosevelt administration in 1933.

Right from the beginning, however, MacArthur had two opposing factions among his staff officers. The chief of the GII, the General Staff Section II, was General Charles A. Willoughby (1892–1972), who had been a staff officer to General MacArthur since 1940 in the Philippines. The section was in charge of information and counter-espionage activities. Under this cover, General Willoughby kept contact with former officials of the special secret police of Japan and gathered information imbued with the anti-communist bias of the wartime Japanese police, which accorded with the general's own political views. He also gathered information on what he considered undesirable activities of officials of the Occupation. The information thus collected was sent to the U.S. House of Representatives Un-American Activities Committee and was used for the McCarthyist removal of active New Dealers in the earlier phase of the Occupation.

The Government Section of MacArthur's staff was headed by

Occupation: the American Way of Life as an Imposed Model

General Courtney Whitney (1897–1969), who had been a practising lawyer in the Philippines before the war and was in charge of General MacArthur's financial affairs. In 1940, he returned to military service as a major in the army and directed guerrilla warfare against Japan in the Philippines. In 1943, he was appointed chief of the Government Section of the U.S. Army in the Pacific theatre, and he arrived in Japan with MacArthur on 30 August. Although he was in conflict with General Willoughby, he kept the trust and affection of General MacArthur and was loyal to the general to the end of his life.

Next to General Whitney in the Government Section was Colonel Charles L. Kades (1906–   ). Born in Newburg, New York, he graduated from Cornell University and went to Harvard Law School. In 1931 he became a lawyer in New York. In 1933, he served under the Secretary of the Interior, Harold L. Ickes, in Roosevelt's cabinet. In 1942, he entered military service and served in the European theatre, in charge of civil administration in the former German Occupied Area. He arrived in Japan on 30 August, with the papers on Occupation policies from Washington. With General Whitney, Commander Alfred R. Hussey (1899–   ) and Milo E. Rowell (1903–   ), Kades worked on the original draft of the constitution of Japan, which explicitly stated that Japan would henceforward waive the right to wage war. Kades was active in land reform, the dismantling of financial monopoly groups, and the purge of wartime leaders from responsible official posts. These activities incurred the enmity of General Willoughby, who publicized Kades' relationship with Viscountess Torio Tsuruyo and so forced him to leave Japan. Nevertheless, General MacArthur preserved his paternalistic regard for Kades and left his private financial affairs in his charge.

As a soldier, General MacArthur firmly opposed communism of all kinds and was therefore hawkish in his recommendation on the military move against Soviet Russia and Communist China. He was a conservative with regard to politics within the United States.

With regard to Japan, however, as civil administrator superior to the Emperor of Japan, MacArthur took a paternalistic attitude which entailed the encouragement of reform. His opinion is well expressed in a statement he made after he had left Japan to the U.S. Congress in 1951, that the Japanese were mentally 12 years

3

old. The publication of this statement in Japanese newspapers angered the Japanese, who had by that time come to place full trust in General MacArthur's goodwill toward the Japanese people. There can be no doubt of his goodwill, but it was the goodwill of a full-grown man towards a 12-year-old.

In the beginning, the term of the Occupation was not specified. To the Japanese, it appeared as though the Occupation would last for ever, just as a few years before it had appeared that the war would last for ever. Accordingly, they prepared to adjust themselves to permanent occupation. Most remarkable was the retraining of the bureaucracy. The Occupation functioned as a training centre for the new class of high officials who were to take the helm of state in the years of swift economic growth after the 1960s. The list of Japanese government liaison officials who negotiated with or, more truthfully, took orders directly from the Occupation headquarters is a list of the conservative party leaders and cabinet ministers of the period after 1960. Most of these officials were already in their forties at the beginning of the Occupation but nevertheless strove to learn the English language, so that by the 1960s they could negotiate with U.S. cabinet members without the help of interpreters.

Before the Occupation, the Japanese higher education system was such that few Japanese could speak and write English, or any foreign language, with fluency. It had long been believed that there was a jinx on Japanese officialdom to the effect that an adept in a foreign language would never rise to the highest rank. The jinx was broken with the Occupation and the character of high officialdom has been transformed. The imprint of the U.S. Occupation remains on the officialdom of Japan.

The close link between Japanese officialdom and the Occupation system was a material consequence of the indirect occupation which the U.S. adopted in Japan, in contrast to the Allies' occupation of Germany. The U.S. policy was to make use of the Japanese Emperor and his government as far as they could serve the aims of the U.S. Occupation, although the U.S. Army could demand the replacement of government organs and personnel or take action independently of the Japanese government.

At the beginning there had loomed another possibility which, if realized, would have meant direct occupation. On 3 September

1945, MacArthur was to have made an announcement that the U.S. Army would occupy all of Japan and begin military rule. The announcement was to include three items:

1. U.S. military administration:
2. the replacement of the Japanese judicial system by U.S. military courts;
3. the use of the U.S. Army Note or military currency in Japan.

The Japanese cabinet was notified in advance of the content of the scheduled announcement. Prince Higashikuni's cabinet was thrown into confusion. It was through a juggling of obscure Chinese ideographs that the Japanese government had managed to ease the shock of surrender. In Japanese official documents, and in newspaper and radio announcements, the word 'defeat' had been carefully avoided and the words 'the termination of the war' put in its place. The 'occupation' had been called the 'stationing' of U.S. forces in Japan. If the War Note were to be used in Japan – that is, the dollar to replace the yen as the currency, and military courts to take over – the people would become acutely conscious of the fact of defeat and occupation, placing the government in a very difficult position. For the government had constructed an elaborate pretence to the Japanese people that they had acted wisely in serving the national structure and had brought the long war to an honourable close.

In alarm, Premier Prince Higashikuni sent Okazaki Katsuo (1897–1965), the head of the Liaison Office, to General MacArthur, then quartered in the New Grand Hotel in Yokohama, at midnight. When Okazaki reached the hotel, it was already 1 a.m. He sneaked into the hotel and went into a bedroom, where he found an American whom he mistook for General Sutherland, the Chief of Staff, and appealed to him. After ten minutes of talk he discovered his mistake, and he was finally taken to the Chief of Staff, who said that the telegrams had already been sent to all the depots in Japan and that the announcement was to be made public the next day. But finally General Sutherland saw the importance of Okazaki's objections in the light of the policy dispatched from Washington, and agreed to stop the announcement. Even Okazaki's report could not allay the alarm of the Japanese cabinet, and Foreign Minister Shigemitsu was sent to visit General MacArthur before 9 a.m. that day. All this occurred in the small hours, during which time the whole cabinet stayed awake.

The discrepancy between the Japanese and the English wording of the same facts of surrender and occupation may be attributed not only to the contrivance of Japanese officials but also to the very nature of the U.S. policy of occupation in Japan, which aimed at a 'conditional' unconditional surrender. The ambiguity is rooted in the U.S. policy itself, in the unilateral information of the terms of the Potsdam Declaration as terms of surrender for Japan. Although terms were stated, the demand for unconditional surrender was never openly retracted by the U.S. official sources. For this reason the U.S. Occupation allowed the Japanese use of the terms 'termination of war' and 'stationing of forces' in lieu of 'defeat' and 'occupation', which gave rise to the controversy over the reality of 'unconditional surrender' in Japanese journalism 33 years later.[1]

The link between the Japanese bureaucracy and its U.S. counterpart did not affect the Japanese system for training high officials, which remained as it had been before the war, in spite of the education reform brought about by the directives of the Occupation. The Ministry of Education remained intact, although the Ministry of the Interior, responsible for police control, was abolished during the Occupation. The pyramidal school system, with Tokyo University at the top, remained unscathed, and still operates. The Law Department of Tokyo University is the training ground for those who are to occupy the highest posts of the bureaucracy. The fact that the faculty members of Tokyo University are trained by a system of in-breeding has also not changed. Those who have climbed up the ladder of competitive examination to the Law Department of Tokyo University feel themselves to be a chosen group fit to lead the nation. After they attain the status of government officials, they are not fired until they reach the age of retirement, after which they may accept either high positions in semi-governmental enterprises or seats in parliament as members of the ruling party, assisting former colleagues in the ministries to draw up government policies. The members of parliament who belong to opposition parties cannot

6

hope for such confidential roles. This is the key to the continuity of Japanese government policy throughout the 34 years since the surrender. In the whole history of postwar Japan, there was only a brief period of seven months during which cabinet was not held by this conservative party–high official amalgam. This was during the U.S. Occupation, so even the policy of this government was kept within the general framework set up by the military administration and its continuity was not affected in any serious way.

When these officials, trained in negotiation with the Occupation, came to occupy responsible political positions themselves, they began to speak a new kind of political language. Before and during the war, the political vocabulary was formulated around the concept of national structure, combined according to a pattern set by the Emperor's edicts. The premier's speeches invariably followed this nomenclature. After the Occupation, successive premiers tried to follow the usage of U.S. democracy in their speeches. The premier who succeeded Kishi after the anti-mutual security uprising in May and June 1960 used a new style of political language entirely free of the pre-armistice terminology of national structure. The official policy speeches of Premier Ikeda Hayato began to centre on economic growth, Gross National Product and the standard of living. This could be interpreted as a new political language with which to disguise Japanese economic imperialism in the post-Occupation era. Up to the present, however, as the military budget has been kept at less than 1 per cent of the G.N.P., it is unlikely that such ideas will result in military activity, such as the sending of a gunboat to defend the freedom of Japanese oil tankers to pass the Malacca Straits. The defence of the Japanese standard of living may arouse public opinion as a basis for state action. It will not suffice, however, to transform it into militarism, when it is cut off from the prewar ideology of national structure and strong military armament. The Japanese are not yet accustomed to the idea of the U.S.A. as the fatherland of free citizens which they must defend militarily.

Major reforms, intended to break down the remnants of feudalism in Japan, were undertaken in the earliest phase of the Occupation: the trial of the war criminals, the purge of war leaders, the abolition of the thought police and its public maintenance law, the release of political prisoners, the dissolution

A Cultural History of Postwar Japan

of financial groups, land reform, the Emperor's declaration that he
was human, the draft of the constitution in which Japan gave up
the right to wage war, women's suffrage, and the remodelling of
the school system. Among these reforms the dissolution of
financial groups had little effect, and all the financial groups later
came to be re-established. Land reform, on the other hand,
although it left the holdings of forest and mountains untouched
and was to this extent incomplete, had an enormous effect in
reshaping the Japanese mentality. Farmers developed the mentality of property owners, and began to show a staunch support for
the Conservative Party, which is unchanged to this day. The purge
of the war leaders was intended to remove militarist and ultra-
nationalist leaders from responsible posts in government, industry
and mass communications. The same criteria were loosely interpreted in order to purge all of the central committee members of
the Japanese Communist Party on 6 June 1950. Here the logic of
the purge was distorted.[2] It was coupled with the red purge by the
Occupation directive, as a result of which 20,997 Communists and
Communist sympathizers lost their jobs in government, mass
communications and private enterprises between 1949 and 1951.
In most of these cases the victims, even when erroneously labelled
Communists, did not get back their jobs. Only in universities,
because of the opposition of student movements, the red purge
was carried out in just a few cases.

The Korean War, which started on 25 June 1950, caused the
Occupation authorities to reverse their course, opening the way
for the total rearmament of Japan and putting an end to the
displacement of wartime leaders. One month after the outbreak of
the Korean War, MacArthur's directive caused the rebirth of a
Japanese army, then under the name of the Police Reserve Force.
The use of euphemism in regard to military matters continues to
this day, when what are in fact an army and a navy are still called
'self-defence corps'. This helps, against the wishes of the U.S.
government and of the late General MacArthur, to keep the size
and cost of the armed forces small, or at least smaller than the
United States would like it to be.

As late as June 1948, General Whitney, of the Government
Section, stated that the purge of war leaders should be deemed
permanent, and that in the future the Occupation authorities

8

would hold the Japanese government responsible for complying with the final decision taken on the purge. This statement is in accordance with the Potsdam Declaration which stated: 'There must be eliminated for all time the authority and influence of those who have deceived and misled the people of Japan on world conquest.' Whitney's statement was, however, revoked by the U.S. Government within one year, retracting not only the U.S. occupation policy but the Potsdam Declaration itself. After a few years, the old forces in Japan gathered together and, this time with the support of the United States, reinstated wartime leaders in positions of power. In February 1957, Kishi, who had been a member of the Tōjō cabinet, was appointed the Premier of Japan.

A similar kind of ambiguity was displayed by the opposition groups. After the defeat, as early as 8 December, the Japan Communist Party organized a people's rally to prosecute the war criminals. At the meeting 1,600 names of a wide variety of people were disclosed, including Shidehara, Wakatsuki and Sakomizu, who had done something to criticize the war. Conversely, among the members of the Committee of Prosecutors were people like the poet Tsuboi Shigeharu, who was to be criticized by a younger poet Yoshimoto for his poems in praise of the war. The Communist Party and its followers tended to label as war criminals those who did not follow the party line after the defeat.[3] We may say, borrowing a classification from logic, that the label 'war criminal' was quasi-heterological. (Any word that does not apply to itself is heterological, such as a 'brick', whereas any word which applies to itself is homological, such as 'English'.) The 'war criminal' was likely to be a member of any group which did not include the speaker. From the point of view of the Occupation, the war criminal was a member of the group which did not include the Occupation and the U.S. government.

From 9 December 1945, the national radio broadcasting station began a series called 'This is true', which was supposed to reveal the facts of the Japanese war. It was a programme ordered by the Occupation authorities from NHK. It gave the impression that the Occupation had a monopoly on the truth which had been hidden from the Japanese people. The Japan Communist Party also believed that they had a monopoly on truth, but then, they were still at the stage of welcoming the U.S. Army as the army of liberation and made it an official policy to co-operate with the U.S. Occupation, so they did not openly criticize the details of the 'truth' disclosed by the Occupation. The U.S. Occupation offered the only truth to the Japanese people. There was little left for the Japanese but to co-operate in the spreading of the truth so proclaimed.[4]

There was great confusion in all the major cities, which were not food-producing areas. The most advertised event of the period, the arrest of Kodaira Yoshio (1905–1949) will throw light upon life in this period. Kodaira would go to a railway station and begin to talk to a girl in the ticket queue. He would say to the girl that he had procured a very reliable way of securing food in the country and she would then follow Kodaira to a forest in the country, without going home and informing her parents of this sudden trip. In this way Kodaira raped and murdered seven persons in succession between June and December, 1945. He had acquired a taste for rape and murder as a marine fighting in China in 1927 and 1928. He had been decorated by the government for bravery shown in these battles and returned to Japan as a hero. He murdered his wife's father and was sentenced to 15 years in prison, but the confusion during the last part of the war enabled him to hide his previous criminal record and to serve as a boilerman in the women's dormitory in the naval garment storage section.[5]

Food was the main problem, which made all other problems seem trifles. To the Japanese, the Occupation made a durable impression primarily as a provider of food. Tons of food were 'released' by the Occupation to the people in Japan. Flour, corn and powdered milk were the main items. But on children chocolate and chewing gum made a deeper impression. The memory of these foods, and their association with General MacArthur, forms the basis of a friendliness, generated in the seven years of Occupation, which is still felt by many Japanese living today.

Along with the provision of food, there was health care. After the long war, especially after the defeat, epidemics of various kinds were expected. The Occupation handled the problem of public hygiene in a masterly way, which the Japanese could not have expected from their own government. The accomplishment of General Sams and his staff in the field of public health and welfare is probably the most indisputable achievement of the U.S. Occupation of Japan. From 1895 to 1945, the Japanese male enjoyed an average life span of 42 years. In the later phase of the war, this must have been shortened, although we have no adequate statistics. But from 1946 to 1951, the average male life span leaped from 42·8 years to 61 years. The average female life span rose from 51·1 to 64·8 years.

For people at large, the most durable influence of the Occupation was on the Japanese life style, especially with respect to relationships between women and men. Since the 1920s, American movies had influenced the Japanese to a great extent. After four years of war with the United States, during which American movies were not shown in public, there came a flood of them. In addition, the Japanese daily witnessed the gestures of Americans in the streets, at least in the big cities where U.S. soldiers were stationed. They set models for the exchange of gestures between boys and girls. Before and during the war, men usually walked a few steps in front of women. For a man and a woman to walk abreast would have been considered immoral during the war and liable to be questioned by the police box. Now a decisive change took place, at least among those in their twenties at the beginning of the Occupation. The photograph on page 12, taken from an album of Kimura Ihei, the master photographer, will not strike you as anything noteworthy, but to the photographer himself if must have given the impression that a new age had arrived.

First in the area of food, second in the region of life style, especially in male–female relationships, and lastly in the region of the sense of justice, the shift to the new values set by the United States was felt to be a necessity which had to be accepted. But the idea that the new values were the only universally acceptable ones, as the Occupation seemed to assert, was something the Japanese would not readily accept, although they did not openly criticize them.

The ordinary Japanese view of the conquerors was quite different from the conquerors' view of themselves. All the major cities, except Kyoto, had been practically burned down. In Tokyo, the horizon, hidden for many years, could be seen in all directions. Many were living in air-raid shelters; others used drainage pipes to

1   Marunouchi, October 1949 (photo Kimura Ihei)

store their kitchen utensils and even to sleep in.

During the last stage of the war, a novelist recruited for compulsory labour service commented that his way of carrying earth in a crude straw basket seemed like a return to the age of the gods as told in the legend. Our manner of living at the outset of the Occupation had much in common with the ancients.

Lancelot Hogben entitled his history of human communication *From Cave Painting to Comic Strip* (1949), which exactly describes the change in the mode of communication of the Japanese people from 1945 to 1960.[6]

2 Occupation: on the Sense of Justice

The Japanese view of the War Tribunal during the period of its existence differed from their view of it 30 years later. Without confusing these two historical dimensions, one prospective and the other retrospective, as they are called by the sociologist Robert Redfield in *The Little Community*,[7] I shall try to assess the place of the War Tribunal in the mind of the Japanese people.

From the prospective viewpoint, the Japanese had no preconception of the War Crimes Trial. In the discussion over whether Japan should accept the Potsdam Declaration, cabinet ministers and military leaders were given a commentary by Shimoda Takezō (1907–), then the chief of Section One in the Bureau of Treaty of the Ministry of Foreign Affairs. Written on 9 August, it stated that the term 'war criminals' would not refer to the men who had been responsible for causing the war by exerting their power and influence but to those who had violated international law by actions such as ill-treating prisoners of war.[8] The Potsdam Declaration made provision for prosecuting only war criminals of this kind. Taking this memorandum at its face value as the testimony of an expert in foreign affairs, the war leaders of Japan did not consider the possibility of their being prosecuted by the international court in front of the Japanese people.

In a way, in the prospective view, the War Crimes Trial began with a misunderstanding. Among the Japanese people, only a small minority had dissented from the war, and only a still smaller minority of the dissenters had held a plan for the trial of war criminals. The Tokyo War Crimes Trial, formally the International Military Tribunal for the Far East, was set up by General MacArthur in accordance with the Potsdam Declaration. It was a

13

trial of 28 wartime leaders of Japan by eleven Allied nations: the U.S.A., China (Kuomintang), the Philippines, Britain, France, New Zealand, Canada, Australia, the U.S.S.R., India and Holland. The court was opened on 3 May 1946, and closed on 12 November 1948. The death sentences pronounced were carried out on 23 December 1948.

Both prosecution and defence gathered voluminous documents. A total of 4,336 exhibits were admitted as evidence; 419 persons testified in court; 779 persons testified by letter. The transcripts of the court proceedings amounted to 48,412 mimeographed pages in 113 volumes.[9]

Not all of this could have reached the ears of the Japanese people at the time, when newspapers were printed on one sheet of paper, half the size of a modern news-sheet. Although radios were popular, in major cities they had been destroyed with the burning down of homes, and there was no television. Thus the Japanese people heard of the Tokyo War Crimes Trial mainly through gossip. Even so, it presented a mural of the Fifteen Years' War with some highlights. The massacre of Nanking in 1937 and other atrocities committed by the Japanese, well-known to the soldiers who had carried them out, were for the first time revealed to the people at large. They were informed, also, that Joseph B. Keenan (1888–1954), the chief prosecutor and an American, accused the former leaders of Japan in the name of civilization. They were informed that seven of the leaders were hanged and that the Emperor was not called to the court. It was these four things which remained in the memory of the Japanese people.

According to Keenan, in *Crimes against International Law*, written with B. F. Brown, the main purpose of the Tokyo War Crimes Trial was to defend peace and international law, and the punishment of the accused was only a subsidiary purpose.[10] In pursuit of this main purpose, it tried to establish a new category of war crime, which would include the conspiring and carrying out of the invasion of other countries. This was a revolutionary concept, which entailed retroactive law – that is, the labelling as 'criminal' acts which were not criminal when committed. The trial itself had therefore a certain illegality, which it had to disregard.

Many questions arise at this point. In the first place, even granting the need for legal sanctions against invasion, can we

14

expect a trial carried out by representatives of the conquerors to be fair? According to the natural tendency of social psychology, such a trial would probably serve as an outlet for the long pent-up hostility of the war, a modern legal cover for a primitive form of retaliation. This was the general feeling of the Japanese people at the time of the Tokyo Trial, who accepted the justice imposed by the conquerors as a physical necessity.

**2   The accused sit in the dock at the Tokyo War
Crimes Trial, 3 May 1946**

In the second place, if the main purpose of the War Crimes Trial was the defence of international law and peace, the sentences given to the accused should have been only a subsidiary product of the trial. But was this distinction between the main objective and subsidiary objective preserved throughout the trial? Did not the subsidiary objective replace the main objective in the end? The idea of the defence of international law and peace did not make a strong impression on the contemporary Japanese public. What impressed them were the sentences, especially the death sentences pronounced upon the seven war leaders. The Japanese felt that these seven had died as scapegoats; some thought that they had died for the Emperor, some thought for the great many responsible for the war, and some thought for the Japanese people as a whole. As the Tokyo War Crimes Trial was coupled with B class and C class War Crimes Trials conducted in other parts of Japan and outside Japan, the Japanese had the definite impression that the accused were chosen and sentenced to death at random.

The absence of the Emperor at the War Crimes Trial was a relief to most Japanese. At the same time, it was considered a denial of the very logic of the trial for war crimes. This ambiguity is the most important aspect of the Japanese reaction. It was universally understood throughout the war that all orders were given in the name of the Emperor. In the Imperial Instructions to the soldiers, the Emperor admonished: 'Consider an order from your superior as an order from myself.' This instruction was so consistently used in military training that it became a truism that an order given by an immediate superior was understood as an order from the Emperor and was therefore above criticism.

This was reflected in the proceedings of the military court. Orders were ascribed to superior officers, and the highest in command understood the orders to have come from further above, but the Emperor, the source of all orders, was not present at the military court and was above legal indictment. Indicted Japanese military leaders did not hold themselves responsible for the conduct of war. They seldom said that they themselves had decided on any action individually. This was not a subterfuge but a subjective truth, quite true to the practice of Japanese military officers during the wartime. In this, according to Maruyama Masao, the Japanese war leaders differed from those of Nazi Germany.[11]

For political reasons, the Emperor was not called to the court. That gave the War Crimes Trial the character of an offering of scapegoats to the altar of the conquerors in the view of the Japanese people both at the time and today.

The Tokyo War Crimes Trial must be studied in the context of the war crimes trials conducted simultaneously elsewhere in Japan, in Soviet Russia, China, the Dutch East Indies, Burma, Malaya, North Borneo, Hong Kong, Australia, French Indo-China, the Philippines and Guam. The documents were carried away to the respective countries after the Occupation. Of the trial records 30 per cent remain with the Correction Bureau of the

Department of Justice. They contain many instances of unfair trials: for example, Captain Tarumoto Shigeharu, who was sentenced to life imprisonment and later returned to Japan, testifies to the case of Petty Officer Kaneko. Kaneko was told in court by the presiding judge that he had no involvement whatever with the crime of which he was accused but because he had been involved in another case he was to be condemned to death by hanging. The other case, for which he was hanged, was not in his letter of indictment.[12] The many trials conducted in various parts of the Pacific needed a large number of interpreters to deal with the Japanese, and as even today few outside Japan are adept in the Japanese language, we may infer the poor quality of interpreting that the accused must have endured. No wonder so many were indicted and executed for reasons unknown to them.

Another instance is cited by the same Captain Tarumoto. In a courtroom in Singapore, the prosecutor asked the witness, 'Who is the man who ill-treated you?' The man pointed to a man sitting on the third seat in the row. Then the prosecutor asked, 'How do you recognize him?' The witness answered, 'Because he is wearing the number three label.' The answer reveals the collaboration before the trial, in which the prosecution had told the witness to point to the man wearing label number three, a number which he wore only for the purposes of the court. It is well known that there was much ill-treatment of prisoners in Singapore, and that there was even a mass slaughter by the Japanese soldiers. But whether these criminal acts were traced by the War Crimes Trials to the real perpetrators is a matter of doubt.

The total number of Japanese arrested as war criminals at the end of World War II was 10,000; 4,253 were found guilty; 1,068 sentenced to death; 422 were sentenced to life imprisonment; and 2,763 were imprisoned for a limited time. Many of the 1,068 executed wrote final testaments. Although some must have been lost before they reached relatives in Japan, 701 have been collected and published in a volume entitled *Last Testaments of the Century*.[13] Tsurumi Kazuko, who made a cumulative classification allowing overlapping categories, found that 62 out of the 701 letters contained anti-trial sentiment. Of these 62, 13 specifically protested that the charges against them were false.[14] The dominant tone of these last letters may be classified as follows:

**3 War Crimes Trial in a Singapore court-room,
August 1946**

1	Acceptance of execution for the sake of the state	439	62.6%
2	Continued belief in the military aims of Japan	86	12.3%
3	Salvation in religion	80	11.4%
4	Resentment against War Crimes Trial	53	7.5%
5	Renunciation of all wars and any war	24	3.4%
6	Others	19	2.7%

The sociologist Sakuta Keiichi classified the same 701 letters according to the attitudes expressed toward death, and found four types which are, in order of predominance:

**4   War Crimes Trial in Rangoon City Hall,
22 March, 1946**

1. death as a sacrifice,
2. death as the achievement of solidarity with the dead,
3. death as atonement for sin,
4. death as natural death.

Those who saw death as a sacrifice viewed their executions as an incident in the war. The idea of death as the achievement of solidarity with the dead is based upon the ancestor worship that lives on in Japan as the basis of Japanese religious consciousness.[15]

In sum, the War Crimes Trials, even in the most unfair cases, have seldom met with tenacious resentment from the Japanese people, even from the victims themselves. This seems to reveal an aspect of the Japanese tradition and mentality. The trials were accepted like some unavoidable physical calamity. This does not mean, however, that the criterion of justice asserted in the trials was fully accepted.

The immediate reaction to the news of the hanging of the seven wartime leaders tried in the Tokyo Tribunal included the following comment recorded in the Yomiuri newspapers on 13 November 1948, by Kimura Gorō, a 48-year-old physician:

> I hope that trials like this will not be repeated anywhere in the world. For that, however, the equal treatment of races, freedom of trade, and freedom of migration must be established. Without these three principles, a war of invasion will begin again.[16]

This comment stands alone in the Japanese newspapers and magazines of the time, which were monopolized by leftist and progressive opinion leaders who deemed the hanging as a just punishment. A poem by Tsuboi Shigeharu entitled 'Seven Heads' is more representative of the opinions expressed in publications during the Occupation.[17]

In the process of the Tokyo Tribunal, the Indian member, Radharinod B. Pal (1886–1967), wrote a lengthy dissenting opinion, in which he questioned the legitimacy of a tribunal conducted by the victorious power alone. He asserted that the charter of the tribunal did not adequately define war crimes and that the tribunal could try the accused only on charges of war crimes in the strictest sense, such as the mistreatment of prisoners of war and civilians, not on charges of endangering peace and promoting aggression. According to Pal, the prosecution had failed to produce convincing evidence that a conspiracy existed among the Japanese, the Germans and the Italians to achieve world domination. Pal's conclusion was that all the accused be acquitted. He strongly condemned President Truman of the U.S.A. for his decision to use the atomic bombs against Japan, comparing this action to Hitler's policy of genocide. Pal's dissenting opinion at the Tokyo War Crimes Trial was translated into Japanese and published as an independent book.[18]

Among the judges of the Tokyo Trial, Pal alone represented the view of the Third World on the Pacific War of 1941–1945, free of the influence of the Western imperialist countries. The Japanese were living in Third World conditions and would have welcomed Pal's dissenting opinion, had they been able to formulate the problem at the time. But the Japanese political leaders and opinion leaders took sides with either the U.S.A. or Soviet Russia, and their views, as reflected in newspapers and magazines published during the Occupation, did not show a marked appreciation of Pal's dissent in the Tokyo War Crimes Trial.

In 1952, the Occupation was over. In response to the Korean War, the U.S.A. began to support the return of wartime leaders to the arena of politics, economy and defence. As a result of the Korean War, the Japanese economy was able to achieve a recovery undreamt of at the time of the surrender. Japan pulled itself out of the conditions of the Third World, although leaving behind Okinawa which remains today a vital link between the Japanese and the Third World, with the most important portion of the island still under occupation in the form of U.S. military bases.

Looking back over the War Crimes Trials from the age of plenty – that is, from 1960 to the present – we may say that the constitution originally chartered by the Occupation has taken root in Japan during the three decades since the end of the Occupation, in spite of pressure from the U.S.A. to dissolve the pledge which ceded the right to wage war. No poll in the past 30 years has shown a predominant wish on the part of the Japanese people to erase this article from the constitution.[19]

The Tokyo War Crimes Trial, on the other hand, has dwindled into a mere interlude of the Occupation period, between surrender and independence. Its irony has been highlighted by the Vietnam War, which the Japanese viewed as the trial of those who sat in judgment on Japan's Fifteen Years' War in Asia, themselves now trapped by their own ten-year war in Asia. U.S. Ambassadors and other official representatives sent to Japan since the Occupation have made it a custom never to refer to the Tokyo War Crimes Trial in their speeches and public statements. The Tokyo War Crimes Trial has come to be seen as a sort of moral debt to Japan by the U.S. government, which since the beginning of the Korean War in 1950 has consistently supported a more dominant role for the wartime leaders of Japan in Japanese and Asian politics.

The movement to not not only acquit all of the wartime leaders but even to praise what they did produced a book entitled *In support of the Greater East Asian War*, by Hayashi Fusao (1903–1975) in 1964. This book, written by a former influential member of the Association of Tokyo University New Men, asserted that Japan had helped to liberate nations in Asia from the yoke of

21

Western Imperialism. It received wide acclaim in the Japan of the sixties which was regaining confidence amid spectacular economic growth.[20]

In terms of historical causation, Japan's war was one of many factors which brought about independence for the colonial nations in Asia. That does not give us reason to say that Japan worked for the liberation of these colonial nations, for, in the light of Japan's wartime policies and administration in these countries, it is clear that Japan tried to dominate these countries and rule as an imperialist power. It was Japan's defeat by as well as its earlier victory over the Western powers that brought about better opportunities for independence.

Meanwhile, since 1950 the government has come to expect no interference from the U.S.A. in the glorification of the war years for schoolchildren. A textbook compiled by the noted historian Ienaga Saburō (1913–), *A New History of Japan*, was rejected as unsuitable by the Ministry of Education because it presented a gloomy picture of the war years. Ienaga decided to sue the state and won his case at the local court level in 1970, forcing the ministry's decision to be retracted. The trials at higher court levels, however, do not offer a sanguine prospect.[21]

In the wake of the prosperity since 1960 there has been a surge of compassion for the victims of the War Crimes Trials. With this change of atmosphere, Shiroyama Saburō's well-documented novel, *The Sunset Aglow*, 1976, was met with wide acclaim and, in the form of a television drama on the national broadcasting station NHK, influenced millions of Japanese. The title of the English version, *War Criminal, the Life and Death of Hirota Kōki*, reveals the content of the novel.[22] It traces the development of Hirota's career as a professional diplomat, and shows that he did not play any decisive role either in Japan's invasion of China or in Japan's war with the U.S.A. and Britain. Hirota did not present any defence of himself at the War Crimes Trial and went to the scaffold without leaving a last testament. His wife committed suicide prior to her husband's hanging so he could meet his death without concern for the bereaved. She believed that if she had not married Hirota, he would not have been singled out as the only civilian given the death sentence in the Tokyo War Crimes Trial, since it was through his wife that Hirota was connected and remained in association with the major figures of the Japanese rightist movement. This case was considered one of the most flagrant mistakes of the Tokyo War Crimes Trial, about which even the Chief Prosecutor, Keenan, was said to have been sensitive. From the sympathy for Hirota shown through the wide sales of the biographical novel and the popularity of the television drama we may safely infer that the Japanese public in the 1970s and early 1980s greatly distrust the verdicts of the war crimes trials.

An earlier response to the War Crimes Trial was expressed in *Luminous Moss*, a play by Takeda Taijun (1912–1976), published in 1954, with an English version appearing in 1967.[23] The play is about a captain tried for eating the flesh of his crew in order to survive. Asked for his own defence at the trial, the captain only answers in a low voice, 'I am forbearing, forbearing'. Then for all those who could see, both in the courtroom and in the theatre, a halo appears around the head of the captain standing silent in the witness box. This is a literary output expressing the Buddhist sentiment which is an undercurrent beneath the surface of expediency in the Japanese people.

Kinoshita Junji (1914–   ) wrote a play called *Between God and Man*, first staged in 1970 and published in 1972, and in English in 1979.[24] The play is composed of two parts, the first being a collage of the proceedings of the Tokyo War Crimes Trial and the second being a series of fictitious scenes in which the wife of Private Kanohara, hanged by the War Crimes Trial on a South Pacific island, meets his prison mates and his secret lover, who had been a vaudeville actress performing Manzai, which may be called the Master and Servant Dialogue.

In the first part, the prosecutor condemns war criminals with all the vehemence and confidence of one who has brought about the unconditional surrender of Japan and who has already achieved an unshakeable civilization in this world.

In the second part, the wife of the executed man listens to the account of the private's death put together by his prison mates and his secret lover. This presents his execution as an accident brought upon him by the intrigues of his superior officer, who wanted to cover up his own part in the round-up of spies among the natives.

The private tries his best to make clear the injustice, even after the death sentence had been pronounced, by writing English letters to the regional commander. But, when all efforts fail, he remembers how the wife of a native falsely accused of spying and executed by the Japanese Occupation Army had climbed up a tall tree and thrown herself off in front of her young son. The private acquiesces in his own execution with the thought that when such crimes have been committed, someone must atone. Then the vaudevillian, who had been long in the confidence of the private, gives vent to her feelings by coupling the famous last testament of General Tōjō and the last words uttered by the private before his execution, in an extemporaneous street performance expressing her defiance of the fate of victims of the war.

The last testament of General Tōjō was a 31-syllable poem entrusted to his priest in accordance with the customs of a warrior:

> After tomorrow,
> Who is there
> To fear?
> In the Buddha's lap
> I shall sleep peacefully.[25]

Whatever his role in the war, Tōjō fought courageously in the Tokyo War Crimes Trial for his belief that the war was inevitable and just. His last poem expresses his courage and conviction, on the basis of which he could meet his death unburdened by regrets. The vaudevillian couples Tōjō's poem with the fragmentary comments of the private on his way to the place of execution:

> Where
> Does it flow to
> This tiny river?[26]

She repeats these two last testaments in juxtaposition and the curtain falls.

General Tōjō died a courageous death, without acknowledging to the last the misfortunes he had brought upon millions of Chinese, Koreans, Filipinos, Burmese, Japanese and other peoples of the world. Private Kanohara in the play dies knowing that his execution is due to a mistake in legal procedure, but he atones for evils committed by his fellow countrymen. He is unsure why this mistake occurred and how his atonement will bear fruit, an uncertainty expressed in his words:

Where
Does it flow to
This tiny river?

In political terms, Tōjō's words of conviction may seem significant and the words of the private insignificant and ineffectual. Private Kanohara, however, represents the Japanese popular tradition of little men which was not assimilated into the ideology of universal justice expressed by General Tōjō and the prosecutors of the War Crimes Trials.

The last words attributed to Private Kanohara in Kinoshita's play were actually spoken historically by Sergeant Wada Minoru (aged 23 years) from the City of Yawata, Kyūshū. Wada uttered these words to the chaplain as the two crossed a narrow river on their way to the place of execution. Since he left no other testimony, these words were recorded by the chaplain and sent to Wada's relatives in Japan. They were included as one of the 701 letters in *Last Testaments of the Century*, and Kinoshita selected these few words, from the voluminous letters left by the victims, as symbolic of the sentiment of the Japanese without power or position. There was a small foreword to the last words:

I am relieved. I feel my heart is cleansed. I don't know why, but I feel very happy. I am glad because I now know the joy of living for the first time in my life. But parting from all the people I know makes me sad.

Then Wada added:

Where
Does it flow to
This tiny river?

Somehow I feel with Kinoshita that these lines give expression to the religious tradition of the Japanese people. If we disregard this

25

tradition, there will be no politics built upon the spontaneous thought of the Japanese people.

In the 30 years since the war the Emperor has grown into senility in the atmosphere of economic prosperity. In a press interview on television he openly stated that he was not aware of any such thing as responsibility for war, for he was not well versed in literary matters. So he seems to have sided with the Western ideology of technological expediency, disregarding the sentiment of little people and the victims of war.

If we look at the decision-making process during the Fifteen Years' War, from 1931 to 1945, we find that the Emperor's stand was sometimes manifestly against war and sometimes openly in favour of enlarging the war.[27] It is not to be doubted that he made the decision to end the war by surrender. At the same time, the people of Japan, including those who perpetrated the crimes of ill-treatment of prisoners and civilians in the occupied territories, took orders from their superiors in the belief that these were orders from the Emperor himself. The system was constructed that way. A close scrutiny of the records of the war does not suggest the conclusion that the Emperor was not responsible for the war of aggression. But was his role such that he was responsible for the atrocities of war? The complexity of the record does not lend itself to this conclusion.

Since the surrender and to this very day, the Japanese have retained affection and respect for the Emperor, as is shown by polls and surveys.[28] It was therefore wise of the Occupation to retain the Emperor. But by doing so unconditionally, the Occupation paved the way for the belief that governing individuals need not take responsibility for their decisions. If the Emperor had been allowed or advised to retire at some point in the post-occupation years and to entrust mundane politics to a Prince Regent, the idea of responsible government in Japan would have been better served. As it is, the sentiment of the people with regard to the responsibility of the wartime government is a vague distrust connected with the belief that only the unlucky ones were caught and held responsible.

In the town of Nakanojō in Gunma Prefecture, an association was formed of those who were purged as leaders of militarism. The meeting, called the Azuma (East) Society, was set up with the termination of the Occupation in 1952 and continues to this day. Members talk about the memory of the war and the hardship of the days under the purge. In 1961 (the beginning of the time of prosperity for Japan), they set up a stone monument, 2 metres high and 1 metre wide, on the face of which was engraved 'The Monument to the Stupid', intended as a testimony to future generations of the existence of stupid people. This seems to be a truthful expression of the sentiment of local sub-leaders who participated in the Fifteen Years' War.[29]

There is an ambiguity in this symbol of stupidity, which cannot be clarified by interviews. Are these people ashamed of their stupidity? Or are they proud of it? Living thought cannot be expressed by propositions of exact meaning. The symbol contains a belief that the War Crimes Trials and the purge conducted during the U.S. Occupation was a process of random sampling which brought down many unfortunate deserving people. The monument symbolizes distrust of the government of Japan, of the U.S.A. and of other governments.

3 Comics in Postwar Japan

How did the genre which began as an imitation of the U.S. comic strip become so different over 60 years? Comic strips with the rendering of stories in pictures as well as words began in the U.S. towards the turn of the century. In 1893, James Swinnerton's *Little Bears* made its appearance in the *San Francisco Examiner*; in 1895, R. F. Outcoult's *The Yellow Kid* appeared in *The World*. According to Coulton Waugh's *The Comics* (1949), on 16 February 1896, *The World* used yellow ink on the Sunday edition of *The Yellow Kid* and from this was derived the term 'yellow journalism' to refer to sensational reporting.[30] From then on comic strips became a major weapon in the competition between the newspapers of Hearst and Pulitzer. Newspapers tried to attract new households by catching the interest of children with comic strips. Sometimes comic strips bearing the same titles were serialized by two competing newspapers, as in the case of *The Yellow Kid* and *Katzenjammer Kids*.

In 1919, Asahi newspapers sent a reporter by the name of Suzuki Bunshirō (1890–1951) to the Peace Conference at Versailles. On the way he travelled through the U.S.A., where his attention was called to the role of comic strips. He came back to Japan with many samples, which he made use of after his appointment to the post of chief editor of the newly created graphic daily news (later changed to weekly), *Asahi Graph*, in 1923. In this graphic newspaper he began to serialize *Bringing Up Father* by George McManus, which had been serialized since 2 January 1913 in Hearst's *New York American*.[31] It was a story of a henpecked husband, which was quite new to the Japan of the 1920s, and it exercised some influence on marital relationships among upper middle-class city-dwellers in Japan. The hero of the

28

story, Jiggs, has climbed high as a successful businessman, but still hankers after corned beef and cabbage, the favourite food of Irish working men. True to their newly won position, Jigg's wife Maggie will not let him eat corned beef and cabbage, and this proves a source of never-ceasing family conflict. In addition, Jiggs needs contact with his old friends, most of them unsuccessful. The couple have a daughter, Nora, who looks exactly like a Ziegfeld girl, which again set the pattern for beauty in Japan in the 1920s. Mannequins in the department stores showed signs of Westernization just at this period, and this trend, although interrupted by the Fifteen Years' War, continued, and after the Occupation reached the extreme point, where almost all the mannequins in the major department stores were either blonde or brunette. It was only after the 1960s that the Japanese recovery from a long-abiding inferiority complex began to allow mannequins of all varieties, some with black skin and black hair and some with yellow skin and black hair.

Suzuki Bunshirō, the chief editor of the *Asahi Graph*, serialized the first comic strip in Japan, *Shōchan and the Squirrel*. Suzuki conceived the idea of this comic strip while perusing many samples in his travels to Europe and the U.S.A. After his return, he gave his samples to his staff, explained his idea, and wrote out a plan of the first few instalments. One of his staff, a young viscount by the name of Oda Nobutsune, took on the task of continuing the story, and another, Kabashima Katsuichi, adept at pen drawing, accepted the task of illustration.

Shōchan and the Squirrel is the story of a boy named Shōchan who goes with his pet squirrel to an underground world, where he finds little mice pestered by goblins. Shōchan, a courageous boy, fights many big goblins and becomes a great and respected mayor. The story reflects the dreams of any little boy who feels himself oppressed by adults and wishes for a chance to show his prowess and wisdom. The boy was named Shōchan, because Japan was just at that time under the reign of Emperor Taishō, and, 'chan' being a diminutive, Shōchan was a common name for boys born between 1911 and 1925. *Shōchan* made a great hit with city children, and was commercially exploited through the manufacture and sale of a type of cap worn by Shōchan in the comic strip. The Osaka headquarters of the Asahi newspaper company held a free party for all Shōchans in the vicinity of Osaka, and gave away Shōchan caps presented by the hatters' chain stores.[32] A photograph of the party with all the Shōchans in 'Shōchan caps' appeared in both the Asahi newspaper and the *Asahi Graph*, giving great publicity to the Asahi newspaper and the hatters' chain.

This episode shows that mass society was already in existence in January 1925, when the party was held. The mass communication media were already well enough developed to spread news instantly to a wide range of people with the income to buy newspapers and comics and Shōchan caps, the aim of the enterprise.

The illustrator of *Shōchan and the Squirrel*, Kabashima Katsuichi (1888–1965), learned the art of pen drawing by copying the ink illustrations in the *National Geographic Magazine*. Thus, *Shōchan and the Squirrel* shows Western influence in both story and illustrations.

Japan, however, had its own long-standing tradition of cartoons and even narrative comics. The medium was not pen, which was a European import, but brush, which had come from China more than 1,000 years before. There is a natural transition from Chinese ideographs written with a brush to pictures. This can be seen from the diary of Niijima Jō,[33] the first samurai to break the law of his feudal lord and the central government and cross the ocean to study in the late Edo period, a man who cannot be said to have had a special aptitude for drawing. Similar instances of this easy transition can be seen in the journal of Kishida Ginkō,[34] written in the early 1860s when he went to Shanghai as an assistant to Dr Hepburn in compiling the first English–Japanese dictionary. Kishida Ginkō, together with Hamada Hikozō, once a ship-wrecked sailor, was one of the first Japanese to start a newspaper.

The earliest traces of cartoons are found on the back of panels of the Hōryūji Temple built in the Nara Period, one of the oldest wooden buildings extant in the world.[35] In Nara, we find, among the remains of the Buddhist sutras, comic self-portraits drawn by the copyists, who made these self-pursuant quests as relaxation from their tedious task. One cartoon is dated AD745. It is also an example of an easy translation of brushwork from the copying of an ideograph to the spontaneous drawing of a comic figure.

In brushwork also, we have scrolls like the *Scroll of Frolicking*

Animals and the *Origin of Shigisan*, both reputedly the work of Abbot Toba (AD1053–1140), the first cartoonist in Japan.[36] He was born into the aristocracy and went into the priesthood, where he took part in the struggle for power and position, little to do with religion. By the strength of his associations, he was raised to the rank of the Chief Priest of the Tendai Sect, the highest position in the hierarchy of the sect, but quitted this position after occupying it for three days. On his deathbed, his disciples asked him who was going to succeed him as the resident priest of the temple. He answered that it should be decided by wrestling (although the wrestling was to be the arms only style).

The superb *Scroll of Frolicking Animals* calls to mind Walt Disney's animated cartoons of Mickey Mouse and Donald Duck, a point made by an American student when Yashiro Yukio, an art historian, lectured at Harvard in the 1930s.[37] Perhaps there may have been some influence on Disney. The *Origin of Shigisan* scroll shows a bird's-eye view of the hungry people living on the ground from the camera angle of the rice storage flying in the sky to rescue them. In this the scroll can be said to be cinematographic, as well as comical, resembling the comic strips in the present century.

The legend that grew up around the personality of Abbot Toba later gave birth to the school of comic drawing called Toba-e. We will not go into the later development of comic drawing in Japan, except to mention that the great Zen priest Ikkyū (1394–1481) left a series of cartoons of animated skeletons suggestive of Possada in Mexico and of the later Disney cartoons of skeleton dances.[38] Zen Buddhism is compatible with the brewing of comic spirit. Still later, Katsushika Hokusai (1760–1849) painted the Hokusai cartoons, and the serious administrator, Watanabe Kazan (1793–1841) painted cartoons of young pupils playing practical jokes in a country school of the late Tokugawa period.

This pre-Meiji tradition was given a stimulus from the West by the works of cartoonists Charles Wirgman and Georges Ferdinand Bigot, who came over from Europe to portray the Japanese working at Europeanization. They brought to Japan something of the spirit and style of Hogarth and Daumier. This gave rise to a school of cartoonists who painted critical sketches of contemporary events with brushwork reminiscent of the pre-Meiji tradition.

Shōchan and the Squirrel, told and drawn to the pattern set by Western comic strips, was soon followed by works more and more influenced by the pre-Meiji tradition. Although with an interruption during the war years, in the last stage of which no comic strips were allotted space in newspapers, Japanese comic strips have developed independently from their U.S. and European counterparts.

In the postwar period, three factors contributed to their unique character. According to Tominaga Ken'ichi in *The Class Structure of Japan*, Japanese society went through a transformation in the years 1955 to 1975.[39] Owing to the Korean War, the Japanese economy had recovered from World War II by 1955. Since then technological innovation and high economic growth have become marked characteristics.

In 1955, 41.1 per cent of the total working population was engaged in primary industry; 23.8 per cent was involved in secondary industry in 1955, 34.1 per cent in 1974; and 35.1 per cent was involved in tertiary industry in 1955 and 51.8 per cent in 1975. Highly professional occupations accounted for 4.9 per cent in 1955 and for 7.6 per cent in 1975. Those in managerial positions amounted to only 2.1 per cent in 1955 and 4.3 per cent in 1975. Thus in 1975 only 12.8 per cent of people born in the Taishō era could hope for a managerial position when they reached their forties, whereas 16.1 per cent of people born in the early Shōwa era, between 1925 and 1935, could hope for similar positions when they reached their forties in 1975. This eased the atmosphere of depression in the earlier phase of the postwar period and partly accounts for the prevalence of middle-class managers in Japan today. Of course, together with this there has been an increase in the standard of living and also a rise in educational standards, which have been the basis for social discrmination in Japan since the Meiji Period. I shall return later to these changes.

There was a marked change from a primarily agrarian society to a highly industrialized society in the 1960s. In the 1970s, the change became so marked that more than 90 per cent of Japanese questioned in polls considered themselves to belong to the middle class.[40]

No society moves forward in a uniform manner. There were segments of society which were left behind and hard hit by this change. To this group belonged the generation of young cartoon-ists who made their début in the 1960s, and they greatly appealed to readers who were frustrated by this smug social milieu of the 1960s.

There used to be a form of popular art for children called a picture-card show.[41] A picture-card showman would walk the streets, gather children together by the sound of his drum and show a series of attractive picture cards with elocution. The children would buy sweets to eat as they watched the free performance. The stories presented were sometimes heroic, sometimes pathetic or horrible, and occasionally comic and erotic. The pictures were never printed but were all hand drawn. Because they had to compete with the mass communication media, they relied upon a limited number of hand-drawn pictures.

5 Picture-card show (*kamishibai*), photographed by
Kimura Ihei at Komatsugawa, Tokyo, 1956

This picture-card showmanship was common after 1929, when so many were unemployed, until the war years, which provided employment for all, though of a very undesirable kind. After 1945 unemployment rose again; children spent much time on the

33

streets, because homes were shared by a number of families and were lacking in space, and they needed cheap amusement. Sweets were also a coveted rarity. In this period there was a renaissance of the art of picture-card showmanship. It was hard work for both the showmen and the artists. Showmen had to walk the streets or travel by bicycle. Artists worked for 14 or 15 hours a day, drawing pictures and creating stock stories. Their life was quite different from that of professional painters and novelists of the same age, and this constant work developed a different skill. The picture-card show declined after 1955, unable to compete with films, television and confectionery shop chains. Then many of the artists began to draw for the lending libraries, which provided cheap amusement for children and young people who hired books cheaply because they could not afford to buy them.

In 1963 a survey was made of lending bookshops in Kōbe, one of the major cities in western Japan. Two people covered by the study each borrowed 100 books from one of the lending bookshops every month. Both were resident employees in cleaning shops, in their twenties, and had come from farming villages to the city. In the holidays they did not have enough money to go to films or for other expensive pastimes. The owner of the cleaning shop had a television set, but his family would choose the channel. To such young men, borrowing comic books (*manga*) was a temporary citadel of freedom. They read three books a day, 100 in a month. The comic books they read were gruesome and satisfied their desire to compensate for their state of alienation.

To such readers the most appealing author was Shirato Sanpei 1932–), whose publications could be sold at exactly the number of the lending libraries – that is, 5,000.[42] Shirato drew an eight-volume work called *The Fighting Record of the Invisible Organizers of Koga* and a sixteen-volume work, *The Fighting Record of the Invisible Organizers*. In both, he portrays invisible organizers who fight to the death against the oppressive rule of the fief lords. The cartoons take the standpoint of the peasants, the beggars, and the still more discriminated against Buraku people. There is no single hero. The invisible organizers belong to a group, they succeed one another after their deaths, forming group personalities. Shirato believed that the invisible organizers are the driving force of history, not the apparent heroes, who are just pawns and

6 From *The Fighting Record of the Invisible Organizers*, by Shirato Sanpei

Frame 3 – It's a beautiful sky . . .

Frame 4 (*bottom right*) – I seem to have had this sort of experience before . . .

Frame 5 (*left*) – That time too a bird louse flew past my ear, just like this . . .

substitutes. Many invisible organizers were hidden behind Oda Nobunaga, who first unified Japan after several hundred years of confusion, and Akechi Mitsuhide, who attacked and killed him. This viewpoint appealed to leaders of the radical student move-

ment who had been expelled from the Japan Communist Party
when it began to show a marked orderliness in the years of high
economic growth. Shirato's portrayal of the freedom of the
invisible organizers appealed to these readers, who had come to
believe in the freedom to take initiatives at their own risk.

Shirato's artistic style was developed through painting picture-
card shows, which be began at 18 after finishing middle school. It
was influenced by the Ukiyoe of the pre-Meiji period, but, unlike
Ukiyoe, used the techniques of breaking a swift action into many
cuts like a slow-motion film, and of building up suspense and
horror, techniques from the picture-card show. It is a style
permeated with rancour. The abstractions and artificiality do not
seem to be used only for the story's sake, as in the works of many
other cartoonists or even novelists of the same period. Its
biographical root is in Shirato's family history. His father,
Okamoto Tōki, had long been active in the proletarian art
movement as a painter. He was one of those who had had courage
enough to be photographed with the corpse of Kobayashi Takiji,
the leader of the proletarian cultural movement who had been
tortured to death, after it had been returned from the police
station on 20 February 1933. His eldest son, Shirato, was then only
11 months old, and he lived with his parents through the
oppressive years of war. The rancour which overflows in his works
has a long history of grim emotion with which he has lived since his
birth. His work exceeds the bounds of comic strips and can be
called pictorial drama. His portrayal of facets of class strife with
fine distinction between different classes and class personalities is
unique, even outside Japan. He is singular in not glorifying the
oppressed. He portrays the cruel factional strife among the
invisible organizers and the resulting unjust purges and executions. In this there is a deep-seated nihilism in his view of history,
which makes it distinctly different from the official historians and
artists of the Japan Communist Party or of other New Left parties.
It was this nihilism and black rancour which attracted to him, and
to him alone, many of the young live-in employees who had
migrated from farming villages to the city with only the bare
essentials of compulsory education. His brushwork is decidedly
not urbane, but was rather in the tradition of the brushwork of the
pre-Meiji period.

The artist Mizuki Shigeru (1924–   ) also turned to drawing for book-lending chains when the picture-card shows went out of business. He was born in Sakaiminato, in Tottori Prefecture, where he imbibed much folklore in his infancy and early childhood. It was in this same region that Lafcadio Hearn collected folklore for English transcription. After finishing primary school there, Mizuki went to night school in Osaka. Recruited in 1943, he served as a soldier in Rabaul, New Britain Islands, where he lost his left arm in an air attack. After his return to Japan, he begged for alms in his white war patient's clothes on the streets of Tokyo for a time, with other disabled war veterans. In 1950 he decided to draw for picture-card shows with his remaining right arm. In 1956, when the business went out of fashion, he switched to drawing for lending libraries. Most of his representative works were drawn in this period. They were sold at a remarkably low price: one whole book brought Yen 20,000 to Yen 25,000, or $70 to $100 according to the exchange rate of the time.

Mizuki drew many war stories. Among these 'The White Flag', the story of the fall of Iwōjima, is the most important. It was drawn in 1964 in the midst of great prosperity. The story begins when the Commander-in-Chief has already committed suicide. The survivors of the navy and the army hold a conference on what they are to do. An army lieutenant and a navy lieutenant, now the highest in rank remaining on this island, disagree. The navy lieutenant returns to the cave where wounded subordinates are waiting, and says: 'You have fought well. That is enough. Our country would not force you to do more. You have a right to keep on living.'

A non-commissioned officer, who has lost one eye, looks up to his commander and says, 'But . . .'

The officer goes out and waves a white flag to the enemy and gives orders to his men to leave the island by the one motor boat left to them. 'This is an order. Go.'

The non-commissioned officer says again, 'But . . .'

The officer insists and the other bids farewell, saying, 'I shall report you to your parents.'

The officer keeps on waving the white flag. He is shot by the army lieutenant who is of the opinion that all Japanese must fight

to death. This character, the one-eyed soldier who keeps saying
'But . . .' to the officer's order reappears in Mizuki's later works as
the father of *Kitarō of the Grave*. In this work One-eye crawls out
of his grave and gives advice to his son in a time of crisis, living
with him in the period of the greatest economic prosperity in
Japan's history. His son is also one-eyed and, being a ghost, he
does not have to go to school, a characteristic which attracted
children all over Japan when the work was televised.

The hero of Mizuki's stories says 'But . . .' to the war
authorities, the Occupation authorities, and the officials of
economic growth, all filled with confidence just as Mr Keenan, the
Chief Prosecutor, was confident of the civilization by which he
measured and judged the war leaders of Japan. Very few
intellectuals at the time said 'But . . .' to Keenan and other
Occupation spokesmen. Mizuki is one of the few among those who
had doubts, and has kept on saying 'But . . .'. Although he cannot
offer alternatives, he is very sceptical of the cult of science and
technology that forms the basis of the philosophy of technocrats in
Japan today, and asks where this high growth will lead. To express
this doubt, Mizuki drew a four-volume work, *Sanpei the Kappa*, in
1962, in which a boy brought up deep in the mountains plays with a
badger and a *kappa*, an imaginary creature that lives under water.
The *kappa* has been sent from his republic to investigate human
conditions, and to study for six years at a human primary school.
Sanpei and the *kappa* go to school on alternate days, a contract
quite welcome to Sanpei. When Sanpei dies in an accident, the
kappa decides to impersonate Sanpei and lives with Sanpei's
widowed mother. On the day of his graduation from the primary
school, the *kappa* confesses to Sanpei's mother that he is just a
kappa. Sanpei's mother says that she has known it all along and
has been grateful for the *kappa*'s kindness. Now the *kappa* leaves
for his home country. The mountain range is dark against a sky
still lit by the afterglow of sunset. As the *kappa*'s figure dwindles in
the distance, the mother and the badger stand side by side, calling
goodbye.

The four-volume work contains other fantastic adventures of
Sanpei and his *kappa* friend. All through the work there is an
animism that keeps the story alive. It is a product of all the legends
and beliefs rooted in Mizuki's mind since his childhood in

7   From *Sanpei the Kappa*, Vol. 4, by Mizuki Shigeru

**Frame 1 (*right*) – University . . . will they make me
study that long?**

Frame 2 (*left*) – Dad said just primary school would do . . .

Sakaiminato, Tottori. These beliefs were reinforced during his war years in Rabaul, New Britain. In the many months during which the Japanese garrison was blockaded by sea and air and had nothing to do, Mizuki went with other soldiers into the native villages to help with the farming, and to dance and drink together. What the Japanese were doing seemed then quite worthless in contrast to the native way of life. This impression continued to haunt him after he returned to Japan, formed a family and lived in prosperity. The beliefs of his childhood in a Japanese seaside village and those of the natives of the South Pacific islands were fused into one, and took on a trans-historical character better expressed in comic strips than by any other form of artistic expression. On this religious basis Mizuki continues to question the postwar high industrialization and the faith in money prevalent in Japan since the 1960s.

The artist Tsuge Yoshiharu (1937–   ) began to work, immediately after graduating from primary school, in a small factory and then became a live-in delivery boy in a noodle shop. His natural shyness increased to the point where he blushed whenever he was faced with a stranger. In his quest for a job which did not necessitate meeting people, he turned to cartoons. Tsuge began to work for lending libraries, finishing *The White She-Devil* when he was only 15. His style of narrative added something new to the history of *manga*.

In *The Master of Gensenkan*, for example, the hero enters a hotsprings establishment and buys a long-nosed goblin mask for fun. Then the saleswoman in the toy shop says, 'You are just like the master of Gensenkan.'

The present master of the Gensenkan inn had also come to the town as an unknown traveller and bought a goblin mask in this shop. Then he went into an inn where the mistress was deaf and dumb. Gossip had it that he asked the old woman who came to serve him, 'Was the mistress born deaf and dumb?'

'Yes, maybe because of sins she committed in her previous life.'

'Do you believe such a thing?'

'We cannot live without believing it.'

'Why can't you live without believing it?'

'If we did not have a previous existence, we would be like . . .' there she checked herself.

'Like what, do you say?'

'We would be like . . . ghosts.'

The guest went down to the hotsprings where he found the mistress of the house naked. He tried to touch her. She escaped but, after spending a long time in her own room half naked, putting her makeup on, she came to the guest's room. Since then the guest had been the master of Gensenkan.

The stranger now wants to walk toward Gensenkan to lodge there. The old woman at the toy shop tries to stop him, saying: 'You can't do that. Terrible things will happen.'

'What terrible things?'

'Why, you are exactly like the master of Gensenkan, don't you see?'

And another woman says, 'Quick! Someone must go and tell them about this at Gensenkan.'

A harsh wind blows, and the scenery becomes suddenly weird. A crowd of old women gather around the stranger and move together toward Gensenkan. At the entrance of Gensenkan, a man with the same face as the stranger breaks from the grip of the mistress and moves forward to confront him. That is the end.

In this Tsuge tries, as in most of his picture dramas, to grope for images that will enable him to reach the umbilicus of his uncertain existence. That is exactly what the wartime government and the Occupation did not try to do. To ascertain, to the best of one's

40

**8   From *The Master of Gensenkan* by Tsuge
Yoshiharu**

ability, the uncertain ground upon which one supports oneself, this
has been a constant effort for Tsuge in his picture dramas. For this
reason his work had a small range of passionate readers. Their
number soon increased and reached millions. This represents a
reaction against the cult of science promoted by both the
Occupation (for the Occupation government could not for
strategic reasons appeal to Christianity with the Japanese as an
audience and so resorted to this cult of science) and the Japan
Communist Party. Tsuge's expression of this reaction constituted
his principal attraction to youth in the 1960s and 1970s. He became
a symbol of youth culture and also of counter-culture, for young
people at that time felt that they were being subjected to the rule
of another cult of science, practised by rising technocrats.

In addition to the picture-card show and the lending library,
a third factor contributed to the unique character of modern
Japanese comics. This was the emergence of women cartoonists.

Before the war, Japan had virtually no female cartoonists, and immediately following the war there appeared only one, Hasegawa Machiko, whose work I shall discuss in another context in Chapter Seven. In the later period, however, they emerged one by one until by 1974 they formed a force great enough to work a change in the character of the Japanese cartoon. In the years since 1974 the most creative contributors have been women cartoonists.

9　From *Earthward bound . . .* by Takemiya Keiko

Takemiya Keiko and Hagio Moto each showed a fine tactical sense when they experimented in weekly girls' *mangas* with long works – Hagio's *The Clan of Poe* and Takemiya's *The Song of Trees and Wind* – in which homosexuality featured. They were a great success. The main figures are male, and, in the interaction of these male characters, the cartoonists portrayed the attraction and repulsion between young people in a way which no male cartoonists could have done.

A precedent for this may be found in the Takarazuka Girls' Opera, begun in 1913. The opera was invented by an enterprising capitalist, Kobayashi Ichizō, to attract visitors to a hotsprings resort at the terminal station of his newly built private railway which extended from Osaka. His plan was to open a department store at the starting point and a weekend resort at the terminus, and to sell residential land along the line. The Girls' Opera provided girls, who in those days were not permitted to associate with boy friends, with an imaginary association with the stage. The girl actresses played boys' roles much better than male youths of the period, so in a way they were better, gentler and more civilized males. This Takarazuka culture has been inherited by modern female cartoonists. No wonder Ikeda Riyoko's comic strip about the French Revolution, *The Rose of Versailles*, of the seventies was so appropriate to the stage of Takarazuka and made such a great hit as part of the repertoire.

Today there exists a galaxy of women cartoonists. Those noted above are the ones whom I consider to be the most creative. We can add also the names of Kimura Minori and Ōshima Yumiko, who are of the youngest generation, in their late twenties. The combination of humour and the women's rights movement is interesting and promising. In view of the fact that more women will enter employment with the increase in the number of elderly people in society, this range of cartoons will prepare a new social atmosphere.

Among the male cartoonists of the 1970s, Yamagami Tatsuhiko (1947–) is the most controversial. His cartoon creation, Gaki Deka, is an extremely fat, over-fed primary school pupil, whose only interests are money and sex. He has no interest whatever in school, but calls himself the only boy policeman and polices the other children primarily out of financial and sexual interest. Gaki

10 From *Gaki Deka*, Vol. 2, by Yamagami Tatsuhiko. *Gaki Deka* (*right*): You're sentenced to death! *Man* (*left*): What do you mean, death!

Deka's irresponsible and shameless pursuit of his interests seems to give us an image of Japan in relation to South-east Asia and in that way is quite indispensable.

Manga now forms an enormous proportion (about 20 per cent in 1977) of all Japanese publications.[43] There are ten weekly comics, each of which has a circulation of over one million. The most popular, *The Boy Champion Weekly*, sells two million copies (now four million in 1986). Companies which publish comics are thriving, while others verge on bankruptcy. Some actually went bankrupt in 1977, 1978 and 1979.

The change which comics have brought about in the nature of publishing in Japan has been the subject of controversy. The paper of the largest labour organization, Sōhyō, serialized a debate on the topic between Inaba Michio (1927–) and Tsumura Takashi (1948–).[44] Inaba expressed total condemnation and Tsumura enthusiastic support. Inaba is a middle-aged professor of Tokyo University and Tsumura a young freelance critic who dropped out of Waseda University during the university feud. Moreover, Inaba represents the Old Left and Tsumura the New Left. Their differences are thus understandable. The issue was taken up by the national broadcasting station, and a panel discussion of 20 scholars of opposing camps was televised all over Japan in the autumn of 1978.

Just as comics present a problem for the labour movement, they also present a problem for education, from primary school up to university. The sudden increase in university students who read comics has already brought about a radical change in the character of education. According to a statistical analysis by Tominaga Ken'ichi, in 1955, when Japan was on the threshold of high economic growth, 6.9 per cent of Japanese between the ages of 20 and 29 had completed primary school only, 46.5 per cent had completed middle school, 29.8 per cent new system high school (or old system middle school), and 16.8 per cent had been to junior college or university.[45] About twenty years later, in 1975, the same classification shows the following percentages:

Primary school – 0.0%
Middle school – 23.0%
High school – 49.1%
Junior college or university – 27.3%
Unclassified – 0.6%

Before the war, only about 5 per cent of this age group had gone to junior college and university. The change is quite extraordinary.

Since about 1960, professors have been complaining about the students reading comics. In this regard, I personally consider that the student who has read and understood *The Fighting Record of the Invisible Organizers* by Shirato belongs to a very intelligent group in today's university population in Japan. This is a defence of comics but not of university students as a whole.

Today many universities have comic clubs, where students draw pictures and publish them in their own magazines. Even Tokyo University has one, whereas Kyoto University does not yet have one. Waseda University has produced the greatest number of successful cartoonists so far.

Probably, the development of Japanese cartoons away from the trend set by the U.S.A. resulted from the influence of the picture-card show, of lending libraries, and of women cartoonists, as well as from differences in social history.

4 Vaudeville Acts

When Tokugawa Ieyasu entered Tokyo, then known as Edo, in 1590, the place was composed of a fortress and some desolate communities. In twenty years it was transformed into such a lively city that a shipwrecked former governor of the Philippines, Don Rodrigo de Vivero, praised its city planning and wrote that although in exterior appearance houses in Spain were more beautiful, the interiors of the Japanese houses were superior in beauty.[46] Edo then had a population of about 150,000, and in the following hundred years the population grew to more than one million, surpassing London (870,000), Paris (540,000), Vienna (250,000), Moscow (also 250,000) and Berlin (170,000). From the mid-seventeenth century to the mid-nineteenth century, Edo was the largest city in the world outside China.

Half of the city's population were samurai who gathered together from different regions of the country, and officials and guards of the central government. The other half were mostly merchants and artisans. There were few farmers in the city area. Since 1794, following the policy of Matsudaira Sadanobu, an emergency rice stock had been accumulated, which could feed half a million merchants and artisans for half a year. There was a relatively free labour market and also social security for citizens living in Edo.

Terakado Seiken's *The Prosperity of Edo* (1832) records a conversation in the alleys. A mendicant comes home at noon and tells a nun that because of the current inflation he had not been given much rice. He says that thanks to the rice storage they would not starve, but should try to save and economize in case of emergency. Overhearing this conversation, a neighbour shouts from beyond the wall, 'Stop such gloomy talk. When Nakamura

Shikan, the star kabuki actor, left Edo for Osaka, the patrons sent him one hundred ryō in one night, and one thousand ryō in ten days, didn't they? Even if we have to eat porridge at home, we give generously to the actor we patronize. That is the spirit of the Edo citizen for you.'

This conversation coming from poor citizens who depended on aid from the emergency rice store sounds reckless, and it is reckless. It indicates the mentality of the working classes in Edo at that time. Their occupation might have been a poor one but they still took pride in patronizing a kabuki actor or a vaudeville storyteller. Fashions were set by the working class, not by aristocratic samurai or wealthy merchants. That was the spirit of Edo.[47]

News and opinions were exchanged in the public bath houses and the barber shops, of which Shikitei Sanba (1776–1822) has left vivid records in *Ukiyo Buro* (1809) and *Ukiyo Doko* (1813).

An urban sociologist, Isomura Eiichi, has defined the community unit in Edo as the area within which a shout can be heard. Edo was divided into such community units, each of which had a chieftain. Houses were made of wood, bamboo, paper and mortar, quite vulnerable to fire, and they were very small. Streets, accordingly, became a very important part of living quarters, especially in summertime. In particular, streets were the place for children to play and amuse themselves in all seasons. The Japanese are known not to scold their children severely as is done in Europe and the U.S.A. E. S. Morse, who came to Japan in the early Meiji Period and introduced Darwinism and anthropology to Japan, was impressed with this fact, and wondered why Japanese children remained so obedient in spite of this.[48] The reason was an aspect of social life which he overlooked, that is, the self-regulating system which operated among children on the streets in each of the neighbourhood units. Elder sisters and brothers took care of younger members of their families, which tended to be very large, and within the street community elder boys took care of the younger boys and the older girls of the younger girls.

This structure of the city has undergone a transformation. The economic growth of the 1960s has transformed the city's structure and has created serious educational problems. Children no longer have access to small streets and have no free time to associate with one another. They are occupied at tutoring schools after school and are directly controlled by their mothers since families are now small.

Another Western observer of the early Meiji era was impressed by the behaviour of a maid who, when instructed to buy a mackerel, bought a cheaper fish which she said, looked fresher. The observer was surprised by the maid's independence in making a decision,[49] but this, also, was not surprising in view of the fact that maids served in middle-class families for only a brief period in order to learn the art of housekeeping before they became housewives. This custom became popular in the middle of the Tokugawa Period, around the time of Kyōho (1715–1735). The relationship was similar to that between artisans and their apprentices, who expected to become independent artisans after a certain period.

The sense of a common culture shared by both lower and upper classes became prevalent from around that time. This is reflected in the fact that many samurai who rose in the post-Meiji era to the rank of marquis or prince and became elder statesmen married courtesans and prostitutes and appeared on public occasions with their wives. Examples are Prince Itō, many times the premier of Japan, Prince Yamagata, also many times Premier, and Chief of Staff of the army, Marquis Inoue, the Minister of Foreign Affairs, and Count Yamamoto, twice Premier and many times Minister of the Navy. Such a practice was uncommon in Europe and the U.S.A., China, India, Korea and other Asian countries, and could not have existed without this sense of sharing a common culture. These elder statesmen had themselves undergone an apprenticeship, learning menial jobs. Sir Ernest Satow recounts in his memoirs his landing, in 1864, in Chōshū fief, after the war between Britain and Chōshū. He was served an impromptu European meal prepared by the Japanese under the direction of Itō, who procured the materials from war-torn towns and somehow produced recognizably European food.[50] Such skill as a servant and cook must have been rare in a nineteenth-century prime minister. Japan's rise as a modern state could be credited to such men.

Katō Shūichi (1919–   ) has described the salient characteristic of modern Japanese culture as the sharing by everybody of common reading material. In the 1920s, 1930s and 1940s, the president of a company and the janitor would both read the magazine *King*, which sold a million copies. In the 1950s and 1960s, both would read the *Asahi Weekly* or the *Weekly Post*. In the 1970s, both would watch the same NHK Great River Dramas on television every Sunday. This would not be the case in Britain, France or the U.S.A.

The continuing stream of this common culture is a basic reason why more than 90 per cent of Japanese today label themselves as middle class. Standards of living, measured in terms of automobiles, washing machines and colour televisions, cannot alone account for this all-pervading middle-class consciousness since the 1960s. It has its roots in mid-Tokugawa city culture, and, if we trace it further back, in the self-containment of Japan for the last thousand years.

Despite this there does exist a clearly distinguished elite. The line of demarcation does not directly correspond with wealth or class. The elite consists of graduates of the law department of Tokyo University, who tend to obtain key positions in government and industrial management. The farmers well know that they have no equipment to retain the newly given wealth. The realization of their precarious position lay behind the farmers' resistance to the enlargement of the U.S. military base in Tachikawa and the Sanrizuka farmers' resistance against the establishment of an international airport in Narita. Millions of yen would not guarantee a stable livelihood for those who did not have the training and information to make their capital profitable. An enormous amount of cash would dwindle in no time.

The ruling elite also participates in the common culture. Its members, however, are able to manipulate words and ideas imported from more advanced cultures outside Japan as well as the best information gathered by the network of the bureaucracy at their command. The contrast between this elite and the masses has been a long-standing theme in the cultural history of Japan. This theme is reflected in the development of a form of vaudeville amusement called *manzai*, or the dialogue between the Master and the Servant.

According to the folklorist Orikuchi Shinobu (1887–1953), linguistic arts in Japan have their origin in banquet amusements.[51] The stunts performed at banquets are preserved in modern festival dances at local shrines. In these stunts the principal role is that of a guest of honour, a visitor to the house and also to the locality. A local spirit appears and tries clumsily to imitate whatever the guest says, and through this clumsy mimicry resists and contradicts the message of the main guest, which must be obeyed. The performance, however, ends with his capitulation. He becomes silent. The play ends with the wry grimace of the local spirit. This play has special masks, the guest god's being that of an honourable old man (Okina) and the resisting local spirit's a grimacing face (Beshimi), later transformed into the funny face called Hyottoko.

This play took on a fixed form in the time of the establishment of central government in Japan. Officials sent from the central government to local posts gave orders written in Chinese and modelled on Chinese documents. Local people could not properly imitate these or reply in the official language. They obeyed, nevertheless, but with some feeling of grievance and remonstrance. Japan's situation on the periphery of the great universal civilization of China and the sense of inferiority and the need to learn the more advanced ways of a superior civilization have long been a point of common understanding among its people. Even so, the officials who governed local areas by means of an imported official language could not meet the needs of local people. This pattern of representing the political situation has not been outgrown even today.

The banquet entertainment produced specialized performers assuming fixed roles. They came to be called the 'Tayū', who played the role of a master, and the 'Saizō', who played the role of the nitwit servant. At wine brewings they would enact the emergence of good wine, and at the completion of a new house they would enact the emergence of a beautiful and solid house. At New Year they would go to the Emperor's palace, and enact the good events that were to take place that year. From the palace they would go to other houses and repeat their performance. In the *Meigetsuki* of Fujiwara Sadaie, it is recorded in the entry for the sixteenth day of the eleventh month of the year 1200 that a *manzai* came and performed an auspicious greeting.[52] They came from the outcasts and were given special protection by their affiliation with the temples. They did not intermarry with other sections of society. The groups in these quarters came to specialize in

50

11 *Manzai* **performers in the Senshū Scroll,** *Poetry Contest of the Thirty-two Artisans*

sending out *manzai* couples. As many households wanted such feliciations at New Year, the specialist quarters sent *manzai* performers all around the country to make their annual rounds at the beginning of the year. At other times of the year the performers worked as farmers in their own villages.[53]

The heart of the performance was a simple dialogue between the serious character and the nitwit. As time went on, it attracted and assimilated new techniques from other forms of amusement. Especially after the Russo–Japanese War, the age-old custom of the summer dance festival gave a new stimulus to the growth of *manzai*.[54] In summer villages hold communal dance parties; the whole village dances in a ring, and a certain amount of sexual licence is allowed on that night. The master of ceremonies stands on a specially erected tower in the centre of the ring and encourages the dancers, making jokes directed at the villagers. This art of extemporaneous wit was introduced to small vaudeville theatres in the cities of Osaka and Kōbe, which were expanding

12   Mikawa *manzai* in the closing years of the Edo
Period (Tayū on the right, Saizō on the left)

rapidly with the sudden industrialization of Japan. People who in their youth had failed at higher professions such as kabuki actors, soldiers, dentists, officials and bank clerks, or later, bus drivers, movie actors, hairdressers and stewardesses, turned to the lowly beggar's art of *manzai*. With such backgrounds, they introduced mimicries of these professions. Through such autobiographical fragments, they reflected Japanese society at large from the periphery, never falling into the middle-class smugness towards which Japanese society had an innate inclination. In this, the modern *manzai* preserves something of its ancient and medieval character, true to its origin in social stratification.

A curious aspect of the art of *manzai* is that the performance was never a drama. In *manzai*, the performers were always themselves, and they told whatever they wanted to tell as something they had experienced (even if the experiences were invented). In

13   Vaudeville scene in the late Edo Period

this, *manzai* differs from the *rakugo*, the art of telling droll stories, another vaudeville art fostered in the Edo Period. In *rakugo* the stories are presented as tales, not as something that has happened to the teller himself. And as the art of storytelling gained social status in the age of television, all the noted Rakugo specialists came to enjoy a high standard of living, which cut them off from the materials which made up the stuff of their stories such as public bathing houses and communal barracks with shared toilets. An exception was Kokontei Shinshō (1890–1973), who continued to visit the public bathing house, carried on a young man's shoulders, believing that his art would wither if cut off from the roots of his stories.

    Manzai performers could not follow the same development as *rakugo* performers because of the nature of their art. When many film actors, novelists, singers and television talents went into politics and were elected members of the Upper House, four *manzai* performers also became M.P.s. But none of these *manzai* M.P.s entered the ruling Conservative Party. They stayed in parliament as independent critics. This indicates something of the character of *manzai*.

14   Vaudeville scene in the early Meiji Period

At the beginning of the Taishō era, in 1912, Yoshimoto Taizō, a kitchen-ware dealer in Osaka, went bankrupt because he had neglected his business to frequent vaudeville theatres and patronize the performers. He began a new business, building a chain of vaudeville theatres. His wife and his wife's younger brother were talented in management, and in a few years the family had succeeded in a new enterprise of managing talent for vaudeville theatres as well as establishing a chain of small vaudeville theatres all over Osaka. Later this Yoshimoto company came to own a chain of vaudeville theatres in most of the major cities in Japan. Through Yoshimoto's efforts, the small vaudeville theatres born of community life in the city of Edo survived the age of industrialization. The middle Edo Period had something of the character of mass culture. It was now inherited by the mass culture of the industrial age, blossoming in the Taishō Period.

The Yoshimoto Enterprise under the direction of Yoshimoto Taizō, concentrated on acquiring *rakugo* performers. After her husband's death, Taizō's wife, Yoshimoto Sei, took over and made the highlight of the city show the farm girls' dance about catching mudfish (*yasukibushi*). In the Shōwa Period from 1926, Yoshimoto Sei's younger brother, Hayashi Shōnosuke, decided to make *manzai* the centre of the vaudeville acts. In 1925 radio broadcasting began in Japan, which helped the swift growth of *manzai*.

At the time, the sociologist Hasegawa Nyozekan (1875–1969) warned that the development of mass communication like movies, photographic magazines, gramophone records and radio, would bring about a decline also in live arts such as singing and festival dancing in villages and towns, and would in the long run result in the decline of the original (not reproduction) arts. Yoshimoto's programme of preserving small theatres and sending *manzai* performers all over Japan was an effort to counteract the lethargy brought about by the swift development of mechanized forms of communication.

Up to this time, *manzai* performers had learned their techniques through an apprenticeship to veteran *manzai* couples, and jokes were extemporaneous. After 1933, however, two men, Akita Minoru (1905–1977) and Nagaoki Makoto (1904–1976), compiled a catalogue of jokes which could be used as fragments of *manzai* dialogue.[55] In 1931, the Mukden Incident, then known in Japan as the Manchurian Incident, took place, marking the beginning of the Fifteen Years' War. In 1933, due to the pressure of popular sentiment as a reaction to the fighting, the group *tenkō* (apostasy) of the Communist leaders was made public. The result was a mass defection of the rank and file of the leftist movement. Akita and Nagaoki were students of Tokyo University and participants of the leftist movement. They shared a room in a student boarding house, and printed leaflets which they distributed in factories. Akita worked as an organizer of the outlawed leftist Japan Metal Workers Union, under the leadership of Zenkyō (the National Council of Labour Unions of Japan). As he could not publish direct criticism of contemporary social trends, Akita began to write humorous dialogues for publication in commercial magazines. An *Asahi* newspaper reporter then introduced Akita to a *manzai* couple, Yokoyama Entatsu (1896–1971) and Hanabishi Achako (1897–1974), who performed a new type of *manzai* dialogue based upon direct observation of contemporary events. This meeting prepared the way for Akita to become the mastermind of the *manzai* trade for nearly half a century. For some time a sale would be held after vaudeville shows of jokes written by Akita for *manzai* couples. Akita recorded a vast

15 *Manzai* **team Hanabishi Achako** (*left*) **and Yokoyama Entatsu** (*right*)

number of jokes, classified according to form and theme. Part of them were published recently. They consist of little jokes like this:

Conservation between a lady passenger and the captain of a ship:
Lady passenger: I'm afraid of getting seasick. What would you recommend as a meal?
Captain: Eat the cheapest dish on the menu.

This brings out into the open the very thing which the lady has tried to banish from her thoughts: vomiting.

Conversation between two children:
Elder brother: I'm frightened of war.
Little brother: Why are you frightened?
Elder brother: Because you are killed by the enemy.
Little brother: Then I'll be the enemy.

This reveals an angle which the government tried to hide by controlling wartime opinion, with the co-operation of most scholars and writers of the time. *Manzai*, if left unrestricted, inevitably developed a critical viewpoint, at least hypothetically, and had therefore to be suppressed as the war continued, just as there was no room left for cartoons in the later stage of the war.

Akita and Nagaoki worked for Yoshimoto Enterprise but had little to do in the last part of the war. After the war, Nagaoki wrote a comic radio script, *Good-natured Father*, for Hanabishi Achako, which made him the most famous comedian in Japan in the 1950s. Achako's programme began in 1952 and lasted for 14 years. By 1959, it had been listed as the most popular programme on the national network more than 200 times, and Nagaoki was awarded a Note of Thanks.

A contribution was made to the postwar development of *manzai* by two divorced couples, Miyako Chōchō and Nanto Yūji and Kyō Utako and Ōtori Keisuke. Both of these held family counselling programmes on radio and television for many years in the *manzai* style. Before the war, the Japanese, obedient to government-enforced morality, were severe with divorced women. There has been a decisive change since the defeat. Miyako Chōchō and Nanto Yūji, a *manzai* couple, began a marriage counselling show in which they talked with couples and added their own extemporaneous comments on the basis of their experience as an old

16 Miyako Chōchō (*left*) and Nanto Yūji (*right*)

married couple. It was an innovative use of *manzai* and proved quite popular. After the programme had run for some time, the couple were divorced and Nanto Yūji remarried. In prewar times, the programme would have been discontinued, but public opinion had undergone a change to which the broadcasting company directors were sensitive, and the programme continued after they disclosed their divorce. The public felt that a *manzai* couple who had been through a divorce and could still remain friends were better fitted to listen to the grievances of married life. Chōchō gained greater popularity, and Yūji, her ex-husband, continued to

17   Ōtori Keisuke (*left*) and Kyō Utako (*right*)

play the part of the unworthy partner and to be a foil for his ex-wife.

Chōchō was illiterate, and before her the famous Wakana of the Wakana-Ichirō couple had also been illiterate. Considering the high literacy in Japan since the Taishō Period, the illiteracy of the two greatest female *manzai* stars reveals the position of *manzai* in the hierarchy of popular arts in Japan. *Manzai* has long been a popular art representing the uneducated class. To this class the leaders of the opposition parties, including the Communists, Socialists and the New Left, seem a shadow bureaucracy, closely resembling the ruling bureaucracy. Distrust of the leadership and the expression of the simple needs of the people have character-ized *manzai* from ancient times to the present day.[56]

In 1823 an English man of letters and dramatic critic, John Payne Collier, wrote *Punch and Judy*, in which he traced the lineage of Punch back to the devil of medieval religious drama, and through him further to characters in pre-Christian Greek mythology.[57] Since his introduction to England from Holland by William of Orange in 1688, Punch has for three hundred years been a symbol of the evil man, and the cheerful evil man at that,

59

and has encouraged the English to distrust official proclamations, made from time to time, that all was well. Punch helped to preserve the idea that there existed cheerful evil men working evil, and to preserve a spirit critical of the general political situation.

In contrast to Punch, the *manzai* couple stood for the inarticulate wisdom of the ignorant which is again and again crushed by the articulate wisdom of officials, but nevertheless perseveres. It is like a *genius loci* asserting itself in spite of the yoke of universalization imposed for 2,000 years. During the Occupation, I heard the following *manzai* joke:

> *Man* (boasting): 'Inu' is 'dog' in English.
> *Woman*: My, you know English well.
> *Man*: I had a university education. Of course I know.
> *Woman*: What about 'neko' then?
> *Man*: 'Cat.' It's easy.
> *Woman*: Really you are marvellous. What about cow?
> *Man*: Eh, eh, cow is eh . . . 'Niik' (*niku* means 'meat' in Japanese).

The man's ignorance is revealed to the audience, and woman and man, facing the reality of their ignorance, promise each other to talk henceforth without pretence. This was produced at a time when Japanese who knew English had a higher social status. The audience is drawn into a fictitious world. Today men are trained to be and work like machines, and to acquire a machine-like accuracy. 'The Manzai' is a criticism of such machine-like skill as valued and practised by the ruling bureaucracy.[58]

18 *The Manzai* **performance by the Two Beats (Tsū Biito): Biito Takeshi (***left***) and Biito Kiyoshi (***right***)**

5 Legends of Common Culture

I have argued that cartoons and vaudeville dialogue occupy a place at the periphery of common culture in Japan and criticize the all-pervading middle-class smugness of the era of economic prosperity from their particular vantage point. I have discussed why Japanese comic strips, which began as an imitation of their U.S. counter-part, deviated from the U.S. pattern and developed into an art form which can voice resentment and criticism, and suggested that picture-card showmanship and the lending libraries were a crucial influence. I turn now to mainstream common culture, as represented by the Great River Drama on television.

Television was introduced to Japan on 1 February 1953, one year after the termination of the U.S. Occupation of the main islands of Japan.[59] There were then, due to the Korean War, signs of swift economic recovery. Television would have been a dangerous weapon for the ruling class to give to people, had it not been for the economic recovery brought about by the Korean War. As it was, only once in its history did television accelerate resentment against the government. This was during the May and June protest of 1960, when people were informed of round-the-clock developments in parliament and left their supper tables to join the demonstration. I can recall no other instance of television helping to organize mass resentment against the government. During the Vietnam War, Japanese television, on the whole, took a critical stand and sided with demonstrators against the Japanese government's co-operation with U.S. policy, but the major target of their criticism was U.S. policy and not the Japanese government itself. In the main, television in Japan has expressed the contentment of the people at large.

62

Table 1: *Changes in Number of TV Reception Contracts with NHK, 1954–1982*

Year	No. of contracts at end of TV year* (in 000s)	Percentage of TV ownership (%)**
1954	53	0.3
1955	166	0.9
1956	419	2.3
1957	909	5.1
1958	1,982	11.0
1959	4,149	23.1
1960	6,860	33.2
1961	10,222	49.5
1962	13,379	64.8
1963	15,663	75.9
1964	17,132	83.0
1965	18,224	75.6
1966	19,247	79.8
1967	20,270	84.2
1968	21,221	88.1
1969	22,088	91.7
1970	22,819	94.8
1971	23,520	84.4
1972	24,433	87.0
1973	24,925	88.7
1974	25,753	91.7
1975	26,545	82.6
1976	27,059	84.2
1977	27,773	86.4
1978	28,394	88.3
1979	28,932	90.0
1980	29,263	81.3
1981	29,789	82.7
1982	30,403	84.4

Notes:
* 1954–1961: number of TV licences (i.e. licences issued specifically for reception of TV broadcasts).
1962–1967: number of Type A licences (which included reception of TV broadcasts).
After 1968: the sum of ordinary licences (which exclude colour TV reception) and colour TV licences.
** While acknowledging the considerable difficulty of ascertaining rates of TV ownership, these calculations have been based on the total number of households appearing in national censuses since 1950.

In 1953 there were 1,000 television sets in Japan. They were located mainly in big restaurants and tea houses, where people went to watch television. In 1979, 27 million families owned television sets. Thus 95.3 per cent of Japanese have access to television in their homes while some families have three to four television sets at home, one for each member of the family. Why so many? Is it not too much of a luxury?

According to a poll only 5.9 per cent of Japanese consider colour television unnecessary to their lives. In contrast, 20.7 per cent of U.S. citizens, 25.1 per cent of Canadians, and 33.9 per cent of the British consider colour television unnecessary to their lives (these figures are based on a world survey conducted in 1979 and published on 1 January 1980 in the *Yomiuri* newspapers).

From the time of the Meiji Restoration until the end of the Fifteen Years' War, in an ordinary citizen's life there had been many tests of loyalty by which undesirable subjects were exposed and rejected. After the surrender and during the Occupation, there was a span of time during which there were very few of these loyalty tests. Each family was no longer required to place a Japanese flag in front of the house to prove to the neighbourhood that it was the house of a loyal citizen. Children brought up during the Occupation did not recognize the Japanese flag when it was hoisted on the top of public buildings at the end of the Occupation. When the national anthem, *Kimi ga yo*, was sung again, many primary schoolchildren recognized it only as a sumō wrestling song because it had only been played on the closing day of formal wrestling matches. In 1980, fewer than one-tenth of the houses in Tokyo flew a Japanese flag on national holidays.

National feeling had to be expressed in postwar Japan with other means than the national flag, the national anthem, the Imperial Edicts, and compulsory military training. In the post-Occupation period, especially after Japan had entered its period of swift economic growth, the television broadcasting of a song contest by NHK Television at the close of the year seems to have been a major national symbol.

Kimura Tsunehisa, a photo cartoonist, had a keen sense of this function of the song contest as early as 1970. He combined NHK Television's national advertisement with a recruitment advertisement by the U.S.A. and used it on the front of the newly erected NHK national broadcasting station.

In 1980, ten years after the photo-montage shown opposite, the

19 The NHK Song Contest of 1953. After this year, the contest came to be held on New Year's Eve, rather than in the New Year.

20 Photomontage by Kimura Tsunehisa

NHK Song Contest was still the most popular television programme of the year. Many Japanese still visit the Meiji Shrine for the New Year ceremony, but the overwhelming majority spend the last hours of the year watching the NHK Song Contest on television with their families. This forms the final impression of the year that they have experienced, and the star singers of Japan are their chosen champions. In 1978, the programme had 77 per cent in the popularity rating.[60]

21   NHK End of Year Song Contest, 1982

Other popular programmes are the NHK serialized dramas, which occupy 15 minutes each morning and roughly correspond to the four seasons of the year, and NHK Great River Dramas which continue throughout the year on Sunday evenings. These television dramas, which we will come back to later, should be seen in the context of the history of film in Japan. Here, as an interlude, we will make a brief detour to the history of movies in Japan.

Edison's cinematograph was first introduced to Japan in 1897, and was shown in Osaka on 15 February of the same year. The first movie made in Japan was shown in Tokyo, at the Kabukiza Theatre on 20 June 1899. But it was in the Taishō Period that movies became part of Tokyo citizens' lives. This was the age of silent movies. There emerged professional 'live talkers' who would accompany the silent scenes. They used colloquial Japanese, putting in whatever they felt fitted the occasion. Ōkura Mitsugu (1899–   ) became an independent 'live talker' in 1912, when he was only 13, and by the time he was 18 he was earning Yen 300 a month, enough to support ten families. He formed his own movie company with the money he saved.

'Live talkers' served to fit Western movies into the context of the everyday life of Japanese city dwellers in the 1910s. Movie makers in Japan, however, were not satisfied by such a compromise. True to the ideal of perfect imitation characteristic of the Taishō Period, they sought to establish, alongside their studios, a training centre for movie actors and actresses, with Osanai Kaoru (1881–1928) at its head. The actors were required to follow the example of modern living – how to sit on a Western chair, how to walk in Western attire, how to use a knife and fork – set by Western movies and seen and closely scrutinized by the public. When the school was established, Osanai invited Slavina to be chief of the acting division and to teach students how to dress, sit, eat and walk. Slavina, formerly Countess Ludovskaya, had escaped to Japan from Russia after the Revolution of 1917, and her daughter, Kitty Slavina, became the first Japanese movie star.

In his autobiography, Yanagita Kunio (1875–1962) recalls a relative who taught the use of the spear.[61] Anyone could tell that this man was good at handling a spear, because he always stood with his waist conspicuously low. For this reason he looked short, but his posture was not considered remarkable since it was common among the samurai class. It was only after 1906 (that is, after the Sino–Japanese War) that such a posture came to be a laughing stock. Yanagita went to Tokyo Station just after it was built in 1914, and saw a throng of young men at the exit, all with their long legs shown off in well-pressed trousers. He was impressed by the fact that a new age had arrived. To keep the balance in the lower part of the body and to put a strain on one's belly was the ideal posture of a samurai when sitting, standing or walking. But now the fashion for young men was to stand straight and to look so light that a breath of wind could blow them away.

Yanagita does not mention farmers. But farmers, who constituted the majority of the people, also kept the balance in the lower part of their bodies so they could crouch at their work in the fields. Movie makers, as the leaders of fashion, had the task of training new stars in the new posture.

In the following Shōwa Period, 15 years of war encouraged a practical, mechanized way of life. After the surrender, the fashions set by the Occupation remained for some time, although only as unattainable goals. But the following swift economic growth drove the agricultural population into factories and service areas so that by 1960 the majority of Japanese lived in an urban environment. Television dramas, therefore, unlike the early movies of the 1910s and 1920s, do not introduce new ways of life, but reflect actual living conditions. In this way the Great River Dramas on television differ in function from movies of the early period.

22 NHK Great River Drama *Akō Rōshi*, on the theme of the Forty-seven Faithful Retainers (1964)

Certain themes are constantly repeated in television dramas. The avenging of their lord by 47 faithful retainers led by Ōishi Kuranosuke, called Chūshingura, had long been a favourite theme for both kabuki plays and movies. It was prohibited by the Occupation, however, and was not seen in the theatres for some time. It suggested too bluntly the possibility of a plot against the life of General MacArthur by the subordinates of the generals who had been hanged.

Since Japan's main islands recovered their independence, there has been a revival of the cult of hard work – a workaholism or, rather, a work-ism. At first the ideal was a desperate bread-winner's striving for the sake of his family. Gradually it became the hard-working mood prevailing in a company. Through this cult of hard work as practised in the collective enterprise, Japan succeeded in climbing the ladder of success in the international market. For this prevailing mood, the Chūshingura, or team of 47 faithful retainers, was a fitting symbol. In the Great River Dramas on NHK television the 47 faithful were used more than once by different script writers and won high popularity ratings.

In contrast to the prewar years, generals, admirals and prime ministers did not feature much in the minds of the people. Those who attracted the genuine respect of the Japanese people as a whole were baseball players, like Ō, Nagashima, and Harimoto, who worked hard for their teams to win in the pennant race, and singers, like Misora Hibari and Miyako Harumi, who rose from the lower station of society to the highest through talent and hard work. Of these Ō (Chinese), Harimoto (Korean) and Miyako (Korean) are not Japanese. They thus also broke down a barrier of social discrimination by winning respect in the fields of sport and entertainment. The imperial system was given television attention when the Crown Prince married a plebeian girl, but with this exception it has not functioned as a source of popular solidarity. It was the heroes of baseball and popular song who daily contributed through the medium of television to the sense of satisfaction in being Japanese in the 1960s and 1970s. The climax of this sense of solidarity was the NHK Song Contest, the closing television show of the year, in which not only major singers but also major movie actors and sportsmen form the committee to rate the songs and determine the winning team.

All this is part of a mechanism which produces unity – in fact, too much unity. Devices to counteract this trend towards unity are found in the comic arts, especially *manga* and the vaudeville dialogue of the Master and the Servant, *manzai*, whose aim it is to aggravate discord in the team and to make the work of the team a laughing stock and an object of criticism. According to the pattern set by the story of the 47 faithful, there is no room for criticizing the aim of the communal enterprise. It parallels the case of humble clerks employed by a company, who are dedicated to the task of increasing the company's sales. *Manzai* and comics hint at the possibility of criticizing such communal aims, including national aims. They thereby criticize the world of mass media in Japan dedicated to economic expansion and restrain it from resorting to military means to back it up.[62]

Apart from the story of the 47 faithful, which took place in the middle Edo Period, the most popular Great River Dramas have been set in the period of the Meiji Restoration or of the Fifteen Years' War. The public has found something worthy of contemplation in these two periods.[63]

The NHK morning dramas, each televised for 15 minutes at breakfast time for about four months, provide some contemporary drama concerned with the life and death of a modern boy or girl. Almost all of these dramas incorporate the Great Earthquake of 1923 and the Great War of 1931–1945, each incident serving as a turning point in the formation of the hero's or heroine's character. For those who have grown up in twentieth-century Japan, the inclusion of these two experiences, especially the Fifteen Years' War, was essential. Without drawing this in, the mural of contemporary Japan would have no unity of design. Although the ruling party and the government were consistent in their efforts to keep the Fifteen Years' War from public scrutiny, they could not prevent the government-sponsored NHK's Great River Dramas from always being concerned with the facts of the Fifteen Years' War. Otherwise the dramas would not hang together.

The Evening Star, Hatoko's Sea and *Weathercock* all depict the role the war played in the ordinary citizen's life. All imply that the war brought little but disaster and ended in catastrophe. The Meiji Restoration had long been stereotyped in prewar government propaganda to glorify members of the Meiji government. Men

23 *Niji* (The Rainbow) (1970), portraying an
ordinary housewife who cheerfully lives through the
hard times spanning the prewar and postwar periods,
while performing the role of a dutiful daughter-in-law
bringing up her children

such as Takano Chōei, who had little to do with Emperor worship,
were made martyrs of the Emperor cult. Japan's surrender and
subsequent occupation freed writers from identifying the Meiji
Restoration with the Meiji government. They came to see the
Meiji Restoration as a process much larger in scope and
conception than the Meiji government which was its final product.

Shiba Ryōtarō (1923–) is typical of the novelists who have
written Great River Dramas on the theme of the Meiji Restoration.[64] In many of his novels he chose as the principal characters
men who died before the Restoration actually took place and
whose design for the future did not exactly coincide with Meiji
Japan, such as Sakamoto Ryōma, Yoshida Torajirō, Takasugi
Shinsaku, Ōmura Masujirō, Saigō Takamori, Etō Shinpei and
Shiba Ryōkai. Even when he set a novel during the Russo–
Japanese War of 1904–1905, he chose principal characters like
General Nogi and General Kodama, who carried through to the

71

24 *Ai yori aoku* **(Bluer than Indigo) (1972) – about a girl who marries in the middle of the Pacific War, is widowed at 18, and her unflagging struggle to survive during and after the war with her son.**

25 *Hatoko no Umi* **(Hatoko's Sea) (1974). Thirty years of postwar Japan is portrayed through this story of a girl, told from the time she was orphaned in the war and wandered into a beautiful port on the Inland Sea.**

26 *Kumo no Jūtan* (Carpet of Clouds) (1976) portrays
the stormy life of a woman in the Taishō and Shōwa
periods who tried to realize her dream of being as free
as a bird.

27 *Kazamidori* (Weathercock) (1977). Set in Taiji
(Wakayama Prefecture) and Kōbe, this drama has a
strong international flavour. It is the story of a woman
who marries a German baker and exerts herself
establishing a bakery, while experiencing the
difficulties of being married to a foreigner.

Meiji era something of the spirit of the dead founders of the Meiji Restoration. General Akiyama Yoshifuru and Admiral Akiyama Saneyuki are exceptional in that they were post-Restoration figures, but these commanders shared the spirit of the Restoration, spending their life force in the Russo–Japanese War and leaving the political arena with the end of the war. Shiba's use of the case of Sakamoto Ryōma is an important example. This man was something of a republican, influenced by the American Revolution. He was so interested in trade that he did not propose himself as a member of the revolutionary government, preferring to travel around the world as a member of a world trading company. It was through this trade that he brought together two prosperous fiefs engaged in ideological conflict and procured from them the English rifles to bring down the feudal Tokugawa regime. Shiba emphasized such seeds of republicanism in the movement which began the Meiji Restoration as a basis for reconsidering the plan finally put forward by the Meiji government. The two Great River Dramas based on Shiba's novels were broadcast in the late 1960s to 1970s. In both *Here Goes Ryōma* and *The Gods of the Flower Seeds*, Shiba tried to portray the movement towards the Meiji Restoration in its process of ferment.

In a highly developed capitalist society, the art form most accessible to the general populace is advertising. Popular arts, therefore, tend to be drawn towards contemporary advertising and to take on its character.

Advertisements, like Bartlett's *Familiar Quotations*, provide standard phrases which can be either used or mocked. Akita Minoru, the mastermind of the vaudeville dialogue, made an elaborate file of jottings from advertisements and turned out a copious number of parodies based upon them. Advertising applies pressure, and parody based on advertising provides the means to free oneself at least momentarily from that pressure. It creates an attitude of independence and opposition to the system. As successors to Akita Minoru, three authors of best-sellers and idols of youth culture – Inoue Hisashi, Itsuki Hiroyuki and Nosaka Akiyuki – produced catch-phrases for advertisements and have twisted them later to a different use.

Suntory, a Japanese whisky manufacturer, had an excellent advertising team, from which there emerged two winners of the

Akutagawa Award, the major prize for novels in Japan, Kaikō Takeshi (1930–) and Yamaguchi Hitomi (1926–).

Kaikō wrote the following advertisement for whisky:

We want to behave like humans.
Drinking Torys whisky, we want to behave like humans.
Because we are humans.

During the period of the most marked economic growth, this advertisement was on the lips of breadwinners throughout Japan, and this short advertising interlude was the most popular television item in Japan at the time, surpassing in coverage even the Great River Dramas of NHK Television.

28

A little earlier in 1961, Kaikō produced the slogan, 'Drink Torys and go to Hawaii.' At that time the Japanese people still had the notion that a trip to Hawaii was an extravagant affair, something which an ordinary citizen would not plan in the course of a normal lifetime. Now, the advertisement says, some drinkers of Torys would be lucky enough to be given travel expenses to Hawaii. To couple a trip to Hawaii with the cheap brand of whisky called Torys would draw a smile from the television watcher for its striking contrast of luxury and economy. But by then, though unnoticed by most of the Japanese, a new era was at the door. Very soon, the inflation in the major cities in Japan was to become so flagrant that it would be cheaper for a newly married

75

トリスを
飲んで
Hawaiiへ
行こう！

トリスウイスキー

29

couple – a clerk and an office girl – to plan a honeymoon in Guam or Hawaii than to spend three to five days in a choice resort hotel in Japan. The value of Torys, which is still a moderately priced whisky in Japan, is no longer so when viewed compared with the cost of living in European countries.

Looking back over this period, during which he produced so many advertising slogans, Kaikō says: 'At that time, I felt the rhythm of the whole age beating within me.'[65] These short advertisements shown on commercial television were the literature of 110 million Japanese.

In the age of monopolistic capitalism, there has been a polarization of literature: popular literature has been increasingly drawn toward commercial advertising, and pure, refined literature towards a kind of science. In the United States, the latter thrives under the auspices of the various foundations, and is therefore under a more indirect patronage by capital than popular literature. Modern Japanese literature, since its humble beginnings, has not developed far in this direction. It is more as the literary output of professors of modern European literature that the erudite branch of the pure novel has prospered in Japan.

A third literary pole is journalism. This form of literature has a prehistory in the Japanese detective novel, which became highly popular after 1960, with the works of older authors such as Matsumoto Seichō (1909–), and younger authors such as Morimura Seiichi (1933–), both of whom produced best-sellers. The total sales of Matsumoto's novels have surpassed 20 million.

The detective novel began in Japan with Kuroiwa Ruikō (1862–1920). *Atrocity*, written in 1889 when Kuroiwa was 27 years old, is an exercise in applied logic. It is divided into three parts, 'Doubt', 'Conjecture' and 'Solution'. The story begins with a corpse and two detectives who try to solve the mystery. One is an empiricist bred in the pre-Meiji police tradition. The other is a rationalist employed by the Meiji government. They work independently, but both reach the same conclusion. The younger detective uses a microscope to guess the nationality of the killer from the wavy hair in the grasp of the dead man. The publication of this mystery story post-dated similar works by Edgar Allan Poe, but preceded the popular detective stories of Conan Doyle.

The story was so unpopular that the author never attempted another, except for a science fiction novel which he wrote towards the end of his life. Instead, he concentrated on the translation of Western novels, which made him famous and enabled him to start a new newspaper, *Yorozuchōhō*. The editorial of this paper, along with Kuroiwa's translation of Western novels, and Sanyūtei Enchō's transcription of a vaudeville ghost story, *Botandōrō* (1884), in the Edo Period tradition, set the pattern for the modern Japanese detective novel.

From this tradition sprang the works of the extremely popular postwar detective novelist, Matsumoto Seichō. Although a group of writers such as Edogawa Ranpo continued the Edgar Allan Poe tradition from the Taishō Period through to the postwar period, it was only after the 1960s that detective stories gained millions of readers and television viewers. The detective in Matsumoto's mysteries has nothing of the laboratory air but rather tries to solve the mystery like a social scientist with field notes. In a way, he carries on his youthful ideal of proletarian literature, which had died under the suppression of the wartime government and was now free from the ideological restraint of the political parties.[66]

After his early success as a mystery writer, Matsumoto went on to write a social history series, in which he tried to solve mysteries of the Occupation period, mysteries of the prewar Japanese government, and mysteries of the ancient governments of Japan. In the occupation series, he tries to take over the role not only of the police but also of journalists in revealing the causes of major incidents such as the murder of 12 bank clerks on 26 January 1948, allegedly committed by the artist Hirasawa Sadamichi. According to Matsumoto, the crime was committed by someone connected with germ warfare, then in the custody of the U.S. Occupation.[67]

Matsumoto's overwhelming popularity is a consequence of the inadequate development of journalism in Japan. Many of the scandals that shook the cabinets during the years of high economic growth, such as the Lockheed bribe case which brought down the Tanaka cabinet,[68] the kidnapping of Kim Dae Chung from a Tokyo hotel, and the bribing of the Japanese Korean lobby by the South Korean government, were exposed in Japan only via the U.S.A.[69] The Japanese journalist Nishiyama Taikichi was arrested for exposing the secret agreement on the mode of payment at the time of the return of Okinawa to Japan in 1972. Japanese journalists withdrew their support from Nishiyama in the subsequent trial when it was revealed that Nishiyama had obtained the news through his amorous relationship with a secretary in the Foreign Office. This impropriety was seen to outweigh the political impropriety of a secret deal on Okinawa.[70] Set against such a background, the success of the mystery writer Matsumoto Seichō in his *Black Fog Series* has been an invaluable service to the history of reporting in Japan.

6 Trends in Popular Songs since the 1960s

In 1875, Izawa Shūji (1851–1917) was sent by the Meiji government to a school in the U.S.A. in order to create a blueprint for instructors of music in Japanese primary schools. He started his official career as a civil engineer and became the headmaster of the teachers' school in Aichi Prefecture at the age of 23. Izawa, then 24 years old, enrolled in an American teachers' school, and of course, did well in all his studies, but failed music. Izawa records in his autobiography that he begged to be allowed to continue music, pleading that it was for this that he had been sent by his government.

After his return to Japan, Izawa reorganized musical education in Japan. Music was to be part of the curriculum in all primary schools, and songs in Japanese were to be sung to Western melodies, transcribed in Western notation, and accompanied by Western instruments, an organ or, preferably, a piano.

Izawa, with the help of his subordinates, including an American adviser, Luther Mason, with whom he had been acquainted in the U.S.A., compiled text books of songs to be used in primary schools. He adapted European melodies for use in his own compositions. The first was a Japanese song about a butterfly sung to a Spanish tune. Few of the Education Ministry officials to whom it was presented approved of the melody, but kindergarten children received it and Mason's violin accompaniment with enthusiasm, and danced to the music. Since the melody was based on five notes, like many Japanese melodies, the song was easy to sing. Encouraged by the success of this experiment, Izawa borrowed melodies from Scottish folk songs which were also based on five notes. Thus a flood of primary school songs and, later,

1 The Butterfly
(Chōchō)

Chō – chō,   chō – chō,   na no ha ni   to – ma-re,

na no ha ni   a – i – ta – ra   sa – ku – ra ni   to – ma re,

sa – ku – ra no   ha – na no   sa – ka – yu – ru   mi – yo ni,

to – ma – re – yo,   a – so – be,   a – so – beyo,   to – ma – re.

'Chōchō' (The Butterfly), *text*: Nomura Akitaru; Spanish folk tune.
(Butterfly, butterfly, come to rest on the rape flower. When you tire of that, rest on the cherry flower. In the royal profusion of cherry blooms, play and rest, rest and play.)

military songs prompted by the Sino–Japanese War and the Russo–Japanese War were introduced to children and the young through the agency of the government.

The original aim was to instil into the young Western music in its pure form. But this presented difficulties in practice, and the result was something of a compromise: the mass production of melodies composed of five notes, skipping the *fa* and *ti* of the seven notes of the Western scale. This is discussed by the historian of music Sonobe Saburō (1904–1980) in his history of popular song in Japan.[71]

Izawa and his advisory group were not the sole originators of this type of composition. Unknown musicians who had been exposed to Western military training songs composed marches in their spare time, one of which came to be known as *Miyasan Miyasan*, or *Tokoton yare-bushi*, adapting currently popular Japanese songs. This was the first Japanese revolutionary march in the Western sense. Its composition was claimed by two army commanders,

80

2 Miyasan
(Tokoton yare-bushi)

♩=108

Mi‒ya‒sa‒n, Mi‒ya‒sa, n,   o‒ n‒ma no ma‒ e ni   hɪ‒ra hi‒ra

A‒ re wa chö‒ te‒ ki se‒ i‒ ba‒tsu se yo to no ni‒shi‒kɪ no

su‒ru no wa na‒n ja‒ ɪ   na. To‒ ko‒ to‒n ya re, to n‒ya re   na.

mi‒ha‒ta ja shɪ ra‒na‒ɪ   ka.

'Tokotonyarebushi' ('Miyasan Miyasan')
(Miyasan, Miyasan, what is that fluttering in front on the
horse? Tokotonyare tonyare na. Why, that is the brocade
banner bidding us to chastise the Imperial enemies.
Tokotonyare tonyare na.)

Ōmura Masujirō and Shinagawa Yajirō, but the true composer
and songwriter are unknown. The song was later adapted by
Gilbert and Sullivan for the operetta *The Mikado*, through which
it has come to enjoy international recognition.

The Japanese musical tradition is characterized by asymmetry –
that is, an avoidance of repetition – according to musicologist
Koizumi Fumio (1927–1983). In this respect it resembles the
musical traditions of Korea and Iran. Iranian music, unlike
Arabian music, which returns at the end to its original form,
changes its form endlessly as it progresses. In the words of
composer Dan Ikuma, Iranian music is like endlessly flowing
water. Japanese music proceeds in a similar way, defying
symmetry of form.[72]

Japanese agrarian work songs, as Koizumi shows,[73] are in
simple duple time, almost never triple time. The reason is traced
to the rhythm of two feet walking on the ground which is required
by agriculture. There was very little use of horses in Japan, which
would have naturally produced triple time, for on horseback the
rider has to resort to triple whereas the march of infantry can
proceed in duple time. Even the Japanese Army in recent times
relied mostly on infantry rather than cavalry, which encouraged
the use of duple metre in the new music of the Meiji Period.

30 Stanislavsky (*left*) as Nanki Poo and Stekel (*right*) as Yum Yum in the operetta *The Mikado*, 1887

The government itself was responsible for the discontinuity of musical tradition between the Edo and the Meiji Periods, by means of music education in schools. Western musical tradition, which was seen as the model, had a pronounced effect after 100 years of existence in Japan. Today, in most major cities in Europe one is likely to find some Japanese in the local orchestra. On the other hand, Koizumi points out, in Japanese music colleges there are few Japanese who can perform on Japanese traditional instruments, but among students who come to study from other parts of the world, there are some specialists who can play with skill instruments such as the *shō* and the *hichiriki*. These foreign students lend their strength to performances of Japan's oldest court music, *gagaku*, creating a situation of reverse cultural borrowing.

There is a widespread belief in Japan, which persists to this day, that only the Japanese can understand Japanese culture. Donald Keene, for example, the historian of Japanese literature, not only knows the Japanese classics better than most Japanese, but is also well versed in modern literature too, and in addition has a thorough intimacy with the Japanese way of life. He writes, however, that he is often admired by Japanese who marvel at his reading Japanese classics, or eating raw fish. It is strange that such outdated reactions still occur. The Japanese themselves are as yet unaware that a new relationship of borrowing and lending, such as with the *shō* and the *hichiriki*, has arisen in Japan, that great changes have taken place in Japanese culture which they cannot keep up with. In actual fact this is not a new situation, but it has been hidden and not taken cognizance of. Surely Japanese culture is not so unique that only the Japanese can fully master it. Kabuki is considered to be representative of Japanese culture, and yet one of the most popular modern kabuki actors, Ichimura Uzaemon XV (1874–1945), was the son of a French general and his Japanese wife. This was not widely known among kabuki circles, but was kept hidden right through the Meiji, Taishō and Shōwa Periods.[74]

Again, one of the top three sumō wrestlers of modern Japan, Taihō, was born of a Russian father and a Japanese mother. This fact too has been hushed up and not generally talked about. Such hushing up supports the belief that only the Japanese can understand Japanese culture. Furthermore, the most popular sumō wrestler today, Takamiyama, was born and bred in Hawaii, and is not Japanese. Kabuki, sumō wrestling, *gagaku*, all these are supposedly the most intricate arts Japanese culture has produced, and yet some of their most prominent practitioners come from outside Japan. If the Japanese were unhindered by prejudice they would recognize that there is some international element in Japanese culture. Soon they will be forced to recognize these historical facts, and when they do they will recognize also that there is something in Japanese culture which is comprehensible, accessible and useful to non-Japanese. This need not be seen as a

**31   Ichimura Uzaemon XV playing *Sukeroku*
(photo: Kimura Ihei)**

sad thing but rather something to be glad about. This all belongs to the future of Japanese culture.

We have looked at the success of the Westernization of Japanese music education. In contrast, the traditional music of pre-Meiji Japan has made a come-back, without people being aware of it, since the sixties, now that the Japanese have achieved a level of industrialization comparable with European countries. To quote Koizumi Fumio in *Kayōkyoku no Ongaku Kōzō* (The Musical Structure of Japanese Popular Songs): ' "Sergeant Pepper", one of the songs sung by Pink Lady (a popular female duo), seems very way out and modern, but is it really so? The composer Togura Shun'ichi has spiced it with considerable delicacy and skill and at first glance it seems that various techniques of Western music are being applied. However, the most vital part of the song, the bare bones of the melody, uses the same scale as our traditional children's songs, basically, a minor scale missing the second and sixth degrees (re and la).' Furthermore, this is very like popular songs of tenth century Japan. Scores of these songs remain in the Konoe family to this day, and show very close similarities to the scale used by the Candies in the song 'Haru Ichiban' (Spring Number One).

32　Takamiyama

Various interpretations can be made. Among other things, we may say that on the level of spontaneous feeling the Japanese people in general, as opposed to the ruling elite of the bureaucracy or intellectuals connected with universities, have freed themselves of the belief that the only real music is Western music.

A brief look at examples of three different groups of songs will illustrate further some of the points made above. The first group is songs in the pre-Meiji tradition of Japanese music. First, the

85

33 Pink Lady

famous 'Chūgoku Chihō no Komoriuta', a lullaby adapted from a traditional song of the Chūgoku region (western Honshū) by Yamada Kōsaku (1886–1965), who modernized it by giving it a new rhythmic feeling and expression. The second example is a work song, 'Hietsukibushi', to be sung while performing the monotonous but rhythmic pounding and hulling of barnyard (deccan) grass. As would be expected from the above discussion, it is in duple time. The song comes from a farming village in the mountains of Kyūshū, and is said to have originated several hundred years ago.

3 Sergeant Pepper
(Peppā Keibu)

'Sergeant Pepper', *text*: Aku Yū, *music*: Tokura Shin'ichi.
(Sergeant Pepper, don't interrupt us. We are just about to have something good. Darling, your words are like an injection, penetrating my heart, they really get me. The purple twilight is like a photo, clearly etched on my heart. Just at that very time, 'You'd better get on home, you two!' Your voice broke our heart in pieces. Sergeant Pepper, don't interrupt us. We are about to have something good.)

4 Spring Number One
(Haru Ichiban)

Allegro

1 Yu-ki ga— to-ke-te ka-wa ni — nat-te na-ga-re-te yu-ki-ma-su,—
2. Ka-ze ga— fu-ı -te a-ta-ta —ka-sa o ha-ko-n-de-kı-ma-shı-ta—

1 tsu-ku-shi—no ko ga ha-zu-ka —-shı-ge ni ka-o o da-shı-ma-su —,mö su-gu
2. do-ko ka —no ko ga to-na - rı — no ko o mu-ka-e ni ki-mashı ˙ - ta, mö su - gu

1 ha — ru de-su ne— ˙˙ , chot-to kı-dot-te mı-ma-se-n ka
2. ha — ru-de-su ne , — ka - re o sa-sot-te mı-ma-se-n ka.

3. Na-i -te-ba-ka-ri i -tat-te — shı-a-wa-se wa ko-na-i ka-ra —

o-mo-i kö— to nu-ı -de— de-ka-ke-ma-se-n ka,— mö su-gu

ha —-ru de -su ne,— ko-ı o shı-te-mı-ma-se-n ka —

'Spring Number One' (The first storm of spring), *text and music*: Hota Yūsuke

(1 The snow has melted and flows away in a river. The new shoots of the field horsetail show their faces shyly.
It's nearly spring.
Why don't you try smartening yourself up a little?

2 The wind blew and brought with it warmth.
Somewhere a boy came to pick up the girl next door.
It's nearly spring.
Why don't you try inviting him?

3 Happiness won't come just from crying all the time.
Why don't you put aside your heavy coat and go outdoors?
It's nearly spring.
Why don't you try making love?)

34 The Candies

The third example is of a type of song called 'Imayō' ('In the modern style'), which were popular 800 years ago. The texts of these songs are to be found in the collection called *Ryōjin Hishō*. This old melody was borrowed as a hymn tune in the early Meiji Period when Christian hymn books were being compiled in Japan. Early hymns made use of traditional tunes in this way, but later it came to be strongly felt that hymns had to have Western tunes to be authentic, and these old tunes dropped out of use. In the same way was discarded in the post-Meiji Period the peculiar method of learning and reading the Bible which had been transmitted by the hidden Christians through the Edo Period. This illuminates from one perspective the character of post-Meiji Japanese Christianity, or more accurately the nature of the culture of Christians in post-Meiji Japan. They firmly believed that only the hymns sung by

5 Lullaby from the Chūgoku region
(Chūgoku chihō no komoriuta)

1. Nen-ne-ko shas-sha-ri-ma-se, ne-ta ko no — ka —-wa-i
sa, o-ki-te-na ku ko no (nen-ko-ro ro) tsu – ra
ni –ku sa, nen – ko-ro-ron, nen – ko - ro-ron.

2. Nen-ne-ko shas-sha –-ri -ma-se, kyō wa nı-jū — go— ni-chi
sa , a-su wa ko –no ko no (nen-ko-ro - ro) mi – ya
ma–i –ri, nen-ko-ro-ron, nen-ko-ro-ron. 3. Mı-ya é ma-ıt – ta
to – ki nan to iu-te — o -ga -mu sa, ıs-sho ko –no
Ko no (nen-ko-ro -ro) ma-me na yo ni, nen-ko-ro-ron, nen-ko-ro-ron.

Lullaby from the Chūgoku region, arranged by Yamada Kōsaku

(1 Go to sleep
A sleeping child is lovable.
A wakeful crying child is ugly.

2 So go to sleep.
This is the twenty-fifth day.
Tomorrow is your first visit to the shrine.

3 So go to sleep.
When we go to the shrine
What shall we pray for?
That this baby grow up to be hard-working all his life.)

6 Traditional Song from Miyazaki
(Hietsukibushi)

'Hietsukibushi' (Traditional song from Miyazaki)

1 Transcription based on performance by local resident, Shiiba Kōnosuke

2 Standard form of Tokyo region.
(On the pepper tree in your garden, I will hang small bells; when you hear them chime, I pray you come outside.)

7 Hymn based on Imayō melody

O - mo - i - i - zu - ru mo ha - zu
A - to na - ki, yu - me no a - to

- ka - shi - ya, Chi - chi no mi - mo - to
o o - i , mu - na - shi - ki sa - chi

o ha - na - re - ki - te. A - men
o ta - no - shi - mi - nu.

Hymn based on Imayō melody
(I am ashamed when I remember I strayed from the Father's presence. I chased a fruitless dream and enjoyed vain happiness. Amen.)
No. 200 in a hymnal published in 1903 (*Repentance and Confession*); no. 245 in the currently used hymnal (*Repentance*), from which this score is taken.

Europeans and Americans were genuine hymns. This is now being questioned by Japanese Christianity and will become a bigger issue in the future.

The second group of songs for consideration are the early Western-style melodies composed in Japan. To this category belongs of course the march song, 'Miyasan Miyasan', which, as discussed earlier, was composed in 1867, and is an early example of the new pentatonic scale based on the major scale minus the fourth and the seventh degrees.

Jumping to the postwar period, we have a children's song composed by Dan Ikuma, called 'Zōsan' (Mr Elephant). In six–eight time, not a traditional metre, it also uses the pentatonic scale minus the fourth and seventh, and is very widely sung amongst today's children.

The next example, 'The Gondola Song' (*Gondora no Uta*), composed in 1915, was used in the final scene of Kurosawa's great film *Ikiru* (Living) (1952). It is sung by a man soon to die of cancer,

8 Mr. Elephant
(Zōsan)

まど みちお 作詞
團 伊玖磨 作曲

1. Zō - san, Zō - san, O – ha-na ga na-ga-i-no ne,
2. Zō - san, Zō - san, Da – a – re ga su-ki na — no,

Sō - yo, ka-a-san mo na -ga-i no yo.

A – no ne, ka-a-san ga su – ki na no yo

'Zōsan', *text*: Mado Michio; *music*: Dan Ikuma
(1 Elephant, elephant,
What a long nose you have!
Yes, my mother's nose is long too.
2 Elephant, elephant,
Who do you like best?
Well, I like my mother best.)

sitting alone on a swing in a park. The song was originally sung in the Japanese stage version of Turgenev's novel, *On the Eve*. The text was written by Yoshii Isamu (1886–1960) and the melody composed by Nakayama Shinpei (1887–1952), a prolific composer of popular and children's songs in Western mode. Russian novels were the rage in Japan at that time and many of them were adapted for the stage, not only in Tokyo but were taken also to all parts of the country by touring theatre troupes. At that very same time musical gramophone recordings were being developed, and samples of these songs could be heard in advance of the plays, which was an aid to their catching on widely in the provinces. Of course their use of the pentatonic scale missing the fourth and seventh degrees, a palatable kind of Western music for the Japanese, also assisted their diffusion.

Even more popular was the song 'Kachūsha no Uta' (Katyusha's Song),[75] composed a year before 'The Gondola Song', also by Nakayama Shinpei, to words by Shimamura Hōgetsu and Sōma

9 The Gondola Song
(Gondora no uta)

I - no-chi— mi - ji — ka-shi,   ko-i se yo— o - to —me, —

A – ka-ki — ku -chi — bi-ru,   a — se-nu— ma ni, —

A –tsu-ki — chi –shi —-o no   hi – e-nu— ma ni, —

A — su no—tsu – ki —-hi no   na —-i mo—-no o —

'The Gondola Song', *text*: Yoshii Isamu; *music*: Nakayama Shinpei
(Life is short, make love, my maiden
Before those red lips fade
Before your warm blood cools
For there may be no more tomorrows for you.)

Gyofū, to be sung by the leading actress Matsui Sumako in the stage adaptation of Tolstoy's *Resurrection*. The extraction of the farewell scene in the form of a song from the play suited Japanese sentimentality, and the song was very widely sung. Nowadays, however, hardly anyone knows that it originated in the stage version of *Resurrection*. It is just a song old men sing when they are drinking. Tolstoy enjoyed great popularity in Japan at the time. When *The Live Corpse*, actually written by Tolstoy for the stage, was first performed in Japan in 1917, Nakayama Shinpei wrote a song for it, 'Sasurai no Uta' (The Wanderer's Song), this time to lyrics by Kitahara Hakushū:

> Shall we go on, shall we return?
> Beneath the Aurora
> Russia is a northern country
> Stretching endlessly to the North.

**35   Shimura Takashi singing 'The Gondola Song' in
the Kurosawa film *Ikiru***

This song too was very widely known and sung.

Next in this group of early Western-style melodies is Narita
Tamezō's (1893–1945) 'Hamabe no Uta' (Song of the Seaside) in
six–eight time, which, while not completely avoiding the fourth
and seventh degrees, in fact basically uses this pentatonic scale.

95

10 Song of the Seaside
(Hamabe no uta)

林 古渓 作詩
成田為三 作曲

Andantino

A -shi-ta- ha-ma -be — o sa--ma →yo-e—-ba ,— mu

—ka-shi -no ko — -to — zo shi- -no — -ba-ru -ru, — Ka

— ze no o — -to yo, ku -mo no sa —ma yo , — yo

—su- ru —na — — -mi — mo, ka — —ı no i -ro mo —

'Song of the Seaside', *poem*: Hayashi Kokei; *music*: Narita
Tamezō.
(In the mornings, when I wander along the seashore, the
things of the past come back to me;
From the sound of the wind, the sight of the clouds,
From the breaking waves, the colour of shells . . .)

11 The Red Dragonfly
(Akatonbo)

ゆるく・おだやかに ♩=60

Yū -ya- ke ko-ya-ke -- no a - ka-to -n - bo

o-wa-re -te mı-ta no -- wa — i -tsu no — hı -- ka

'The Red Dragonfly', *text*: Miki Rofū; *music*: Yamada Kōsaku
(Red dragonfly in the sunset
I saw you from my mother's back
How long ago that was.)

'Akatombo' (The Red Dragonfly) by Yamada Kosaku, on the other hand, uses the pentatonic scale strictly. In three–four time, it is a popular children's song.

12 If you go to the sea . . .
(Umi yukaba)

古 歌
信時 潔 作曲

U – mi – yu ka – ba   mi – zu – ku ka–ba –ne,   Ya

– ma yu–ka — –ba   ku – sa–mu–su ka – ba – ne,   Ō — ki – mi

no   he ni ko–soshi–na – me,   ka — –e – ri–mi wa se–ji

'If you go to the sea . . .', *text*: ancient poem; *music*: Nobutoki Kiyoshi
(If you go to the sea, there are watery corpses; if you go to the mountain there are grassy corpses;
Let us die at the Emperor's side, no matter what the cost.)

The next example, the melancholy 'Umi yukaba' (If you go to the sea) by Nobutoki Kiyoshi (1887–1965), has as its text an ancient poem, and was widely sung during the Second World War, more so than the national anthem, it is said.

'Yuki no furu machi o' (A town where the snow is falling) by Nakata Yoshinao (1923–) was a well-known song in the postwar period. The first part of the song in particular is reminiscent of traditional Japanese scales.

The second group of Western-style songs mostly had some links with traditional scales, making them easy to sing for the Japanese. The third group is quite different. They are from the postwar period, but perhaps they represent a return to the Meiji and Taishō Periods. After the close contact with American culture under the Occupation, and then with the coming of economic recovery, the pace of life changed dramatically, and Western ways penetrated into all areas of everyday life. The melodies in this group cannot be so easily categorized as the first two groups, but

13   A town where the snow is falling
(Yuki no furu machi o)

A town where the snow is falling, *text*: Uchimura Naoya;
music: Nakata Yoshinao
(Through a town where snow is falling
Only memories pass.
These memories, falling down from a distant country,
I shall one day enfold – a warm smile of happiness.)

they do form a new stream. Firstly, 'Kaette kita Yopparai' (The drunk who has come back home), in eight–eight time, utilizes fully the seven-tone major scale. Appearing in 1967 when economic growth was obvious to everyone, it is an abandoned sort of song, its lyrics in bad taste, and it scandalized older people. Children, however, loved it, singing it in buses and so on, while older people hated it.

We can include in this group songs like 'Haru Ichiban' (Spring Number One), discussed above. It was sung by the Candies, a trio of young girls in miniskirts, thoroughly Western in presentation. The melody, however, is a minor scale missing (mostly) the second

14 The drunk who has come back home
(Kaette kita yopparai)

Moderato

O-rawashinj i-mat-ta da,   o-ra washinjimat-ta da,
Na ga i ka ı da n o,   ku mo noka i da n o,
O ra wa yota yo ta to   no bo ri tsuzuke ta da,

o-ra washin-j-i-mat-ta da, te-n-go-ku ni ıtta da.
O ra wano bot ta da, fu — ra fu — ra to,
yat to te n go ku no mo nnı tu ı ta da.

Ten-go-ku yoı to-ko, ı-chı-do wao - i-de, sa-ke wa u-ma-ı shı

nē - chanːwa kı-re - i da, wa, wa, wa· wa.

'The drunk who has come back home', *text*: 'The Folk Parody Gang'; *music*: Katō Kazuhiko; *arranged by* Osabe Masata

(1 I've gone and died, and I'm in heaven.
Refrain: Heaven's a great place, you ought to come and see it. The wine's good, the girls are pretty, Wa, wa, wa-wa!
2 I climbed a long stairway through the clouds, puffing, out of breath.
3 I kept on climbing, dragging one foot after the other, till I arrived at the pearly gates.)

and sixth degrees, a revival of the melodic style of popular songs of the twelfth century and earlier.

To bring the peculiarities of Japanese songs into relief, one should of course really listen to popular songs of Asian countries closely related to but slightly different from Japan, such as *bungawan solo* of Indonesia, and *ariran* of Korea.[76] Another song worthy of mention, frequently sung in Japan, is the Scottish folksong 'Comin' through the rye' The Japanese lyrics are quite different, however. After all, in the Meiji Period the

15 The sky of my home village
(Kokyō no sora)

Yū- zo - ra   ha - re - te,   a - ki - ka - ze   fu - ki,

Tsu-ki - ka - ge   o - chi - te,   su - zu - mu-shi   na - ku,

O - mo - e - ba   tō - shi   ko - kyō   no   so - ra,   a

--a   wa-ga   chi - chi   ha-ha   i - ka - ni   o - wa - su.

'The sky of my home village, *text*: Owada Kenju; Scottish folk
melody
(The evening sky is clear in the autumn breeze,
The moonlight is pouring down, the insects chirp.
It reminds me of the sky of my hometown far away.
Ah, I wonder how my father and mother are.)

Japanese could hardly have sung about a boy catching and kissing
a girl in a field of rye. So it became 'Kokyō no Sora' (The sky of my
home village), a meteorological description about feeling good
under clear skies, and in this form became extensively popular.
Also adapted from the Scottish folk song 'Auld lang syne' is
'Hotaru no Hikari' (The glow of the fireflies). It is always sung at
primary-school graduation ceremonies, and therefore conjures up
nostalgia for school days. So we can see that these European folk
songs are used whenever people gather together, but on different
occasions, and for different purposes.

In the early days, when Izawa Shūji determined the policy that
music education should be along Western lines, a sense of mission
that Western songs must be sung appeared strongly in primary and
middle-school teachers. Therefore the tendency was to be Japanese in textual content and Western in melody, perhaps a kind of

100

16 The glow of fireflies
(Hotaru no hikari)

小学唱歌

Ho – ta –ru no hi –kə — ri, ma – do no yu — ki, Fu

—mi yo-mu tsu – ki —hi ka – sa – ne-tsu -tsu, I –

tsu — shi-ka to -shi mo su – gi no to o a –

ke– te zo, Ke – sa wa wa – ka –re-yu – ku.

'The glow of the fireflies', Primary school song.
(By the glow of fireflies, in the shimmering snowlight at the window,
We have studied hard together for many months and days,
Suddenly the years have passed and the cedar door is opened,
This morning we go our separate ways.)

adaptation of the slogan 'Japanese spirit Western learning' (*Wakon yōsai*). This principle had a restricting effect on the development of Japanese music education.

In 1910, a tragic incident took place in Zushi, near Tokyo, when some middle-school boys died in a boating mishap. There was a girls' middle school nearby, but of course in those days of segregated education boys and girls of this age could not mix freely with each other. They had to pass in the street in silence, recognizing each other's presence only with looks, which probably served to create a much stronger mutual fascination than would have existed otherwise. Anyway, when the schoolboys perished, strong feelings of grief arose among the girls. As a result, the song now known as 'Shichiri ga Hama no Aika' (Elegy of Seven-Mile Beach) was sung at the funeral. The music teacher at the girls' school, Misumi Yōko, immediately on hearing the news of the

17   Elegy of Seven-mile Beach
(Shichiri ga hama no aika)

♩ = 60

Ma — shi-ro-ki   Fu— ji — ne,   mi- do-ri no   E - no-shima,a

— o - gi -mi — -ru   mo,   i - ma wa na - mi — da.   Ka

— e — ra-nu jū   — ni no   o -o- shi -ki   mi- ta — mani   sa

— sa - ge-ma — tsu— ru   mu- ne   to ko — ko — ro.

'Elegy of Seven-Mile Beach', *text*: Misumi Yōko; *music*:
Garden
(When I look up at Fuji's peak, pure white, and at the green
isle of Enoshima,
I am overcome with tears.
To the twelve souls of those we love, who will never return,
we dedicate our hearts and minds.)

boat disaster and the boys' death, is said to have written the poem
and set it to music. She was, however, unable to compose a tune
herself. She was even unable to borrow a Japanese tune. What she
did was borrow a tune by someone, probably an American called
Garden. This was sung at the combined funeral of the boys, amid
the tears of all the students, boys and girls. The song later spread
far beyond the Zushi area to be widely known throughout Japan,
even to the present day. It shows us something of the kind of
relationship which existed between teenage boys and girls way
back in 1910. And furthermore, this taking of a European melody
to express one's natural feelings of mourning provides an episode
which shows clearly the Japanese music culture of the time, and
also the emotions of the Japanese who entrusted their hearts to
this music culture.

102

7 Ordinary Citizens and Citizens' Movements

The words which non-Japanese students of contemporary Japanese find most striking and often the most difficult are words which the Japanese have borrowed from other cultures, because they do not appear in any dictionaries. Even when the original meaning of the word is understood, the meaning is altered in the context of Japanese culture. These words can be said to belong to a world culture, or, more exactly, to an international culture.

One such Japanese word is 'circle'.[77] Its origin may be traced to June 1931, when Kurahara Koreto (1902–   ) borrowed it from a Russian context for use in *NAP*, the organ of the All-Japan Proletarian Arts League (Zen Nihon Musansha Geijutsu Renmei, established in 1928). In this context it was used to designate literary and artistic groups to be organized in factories and labour unions under the direction of the specialist groups belonging to the NAP, which was, in turn, under the direction of the Japan Communist Party.

The NAP was dissolved in October 1931 on the basis of Kurahara Koreto's proposal to form *KOP*, Japan Proletarian Cultural League (Nihon Puroretaria Bunka Renmei), which was established in November of the same year by integrating 12 cultural organizations, not only in the field of the arts but also proletarian scientific organizations. 'Circle' then designated the group's activities in arts as well as science under the supervision of the Communist Party. After the group defection of 1933, these circles also declined and underwent a transformation. Their originator, Kurahara, however, refused *tenkō* all through the war years, in spite of imprisonment. He was arrested in April 1932. After spending eight and a half years in prison, he was released because of his tuberculosis in October 1940, and spent his later years on a sick bed under police supervision.

In the meanwhile, circles, which had become independent of any directives of the Japan Communist Party, continued their activities. Notable among them were the 'World Culture' group and the 'Saturday' group, which had overlapping membership.[78] They were active from 1936 to 1937, in the middle phase of the Fifteen Years' War. They were suppressed during the round up of prominent Communists for their alleged connection with the Communist International, but in fact there was no such connection. They took no orders from the Japan Communist Party, for it no longer operated outside prison.

These two groups reacted to the way in which militarism warped people's lives. The magazine *World Culture* analyzed the situation on a theoretical level. The weekly paper *Saturday* carried comments on daily life. Neither group was bound by ideology. They were issue-oriented. As such they were the forerunners of the citizens' movements after 1960.

Saturday was edited and managed by a movie actor, and copies were circulated in coffee houses in Kyoto. It was a weekly devoted to critical observation of the Japanese life style, and as such it throve as a communication enterprise, leaving some surplus funds in the bank at the time of its suppression.

World Culture included among its contributors economists, sociologists, physicists, philosophers and foreign language teachers. The chief contributor to this magazine, as well as to another weekly paper, was a philosopher, Nakai Masakazu (1900–1952), who concerned himself with the popular front movement on three theoretical levels.

In the first place, he was born and bred in a family tradition of Buddhism in the Shinran Sect in Hiroshima Prefecture, where Buddhist priests had long supported the farmer-merchants' resistance against the political authority of war-lords. He was bound through filial piety to this Buddhist tradition, which gave him a reason to concern himself in local tradition. After release from imprisonment, he became a librarian in his home town of Onomichi, where the city library became the centre of cultural activities among farmers in the postwar period.

In the second place, he was a sportsman, a member of his

college crew. Analysing his experience as a member of the crew, he wrote an article, 'The Structure of the Sportsman's Experience', in which he revealed how the same mood seemed to infect crew members through the accumulation of communal training. A group subjectivity emerged and supported them.

These two experiences created an awareness of group movement as a commune, which is on a different footing from the rational, utilitarian, contractual relationship of a *Gesellschaft*. His idea of a circle is a small *Gesellschaft* supported by a *Gemeinschaft* within it.

In the third place, Nakai developed his theory of the logic of committee work in 1936. He traced the history of models of communication in Western philosophy since ancient times and distinguished three types: dialectics, which developed from conversation; the logic of internal consistency, which developed from meditation; and inductive logic, developed from the wide sharing of experience through the printed medium. Inductive logic diversifies further into functional, mathematical logic, which developed out of highly specialized industrial production, and into the logic of committee work which grew out of a survey of the whole process of industrial production. It aims at a synthesis, a point of view from which one can review, criticize and reconstruct different parts of the thinking process conducted by man. The examples that Nakai cites are all taken from industrial enterprise, but he clearly draws his inspiration from Lenin's political writings, forbidden by the thought police of the time.

With his threefold approach, Nakai saw the communal aspect of the popular movement and also the necessity of committee work which would counterbalance the emotional setback that might result from the rule of the mob to which the popular right wing of the movement is sometimes prone. Rational planning alone might deprive a movement of its spontaneity. A surge of communal emotion might lead to mob rule. A popular movement is always exposed to this dilemma, of which Nakai was aware in his threefold analysis.[79]

World Culture and *Saturday* were both sympathetic to the policy of the Soviet Union. However, due to the historical circumstance which deprived them of any contact with that country, they continued their own popular front movement independently of the

Japan Communist Party and the Communist International. They thus came close to forming a popular front movement based on local Japanese tradition.[80]

After Japan's surrender the Communist leaders who had refused *tenkō* during the long war years returned to leadership. They thought it proper to give directives to the cultural circles that had arisen in the postwar period. After the bloody May Day of 1952, faction fighting within the Communist Party caused them to loosen their grip on the circles, which became more independent. By 1960, the word 'circle' had come to mean any small group of amateurs pursuing some cultural activity, be it artistic or academic. It no longer had the connotation which coupled the word with Communist Party directives.

The way in which this foreign word has taken root in such a short time may be explained by its connection with Japan's village tradition. Tamaki Akira, the agricultural sociologist, has conducted comparative research on agriculture in East Asia. He has found a similar development of self-rule in the control of water in rice paddies in Indonesia and Japan.[81] The formation of a character such as the village chief Tanaka Shōzō (1841–1913) should be understood in this context. He has only just emerged from a half-century's oblivion with the first publication in Japan of his complete works, mostly letters and memoranda. His resurrection may be attributed to the high industrialization since the 1960s. His biography, written in English, is Kenneth Strong's *Ox against the Storm*.[82]

Tanaka was a hard-working young man, and his family had long been known for hard work and selfless devotion to the village cause. His house was very small, like any other house in the village, but his grandfather and father were village chiefs. When his father became the great chief of all the villages in the district, Tanaka Shōzō became chief of his own village at the age of 18. The village belonged to the feudal lord, whose son was shortly to marry. The manager of the lord's household raised a tax from villagers in his domain, ostensibly to pay for the newly erected residence of the married couple. Tanaka Shōzō lodged a protest on behalf of the villagers, claiming that such a tax was not according to the custom of the village. His grounds were solely village conservatism and the customs of self-rule in the village.

Tanaka Shōzō was imprisoned and was only released two years after the Meiji Restoration.

In the Meiji era Tanaka Shōzō rose to the central arena of politics with his election as a member of parliament. He took up the issue of the devastation of farming villages in his home provinces by pollution from a copper refinery which forced many farmers to leave their homes. He failed to receive a hearing and resigned his seat in parliament. He returned to live with the victims in the polluted villages, campaigning for public sympathy until his death. His wife, who remained in Tokyo, helped to organize sympathizers outside the village.

When the industrialization of Japan introduced new diseases and created more victims of pollution, a citizens' movement emerged, rallying around the victims, to protest to private enterprise and the government. With the development of this movement the activists realized that they had a precursor in Tanaka Shōzō. Tanaka's method of returning to the grass-roots and living among the victims, rather than making appeals to the government through political parties and in parliament, was re-evaluated as a method to be inherited by later generations. Tanaka developed a point of view from which he could criticize the state authorities and the bureaucrats in terms of village tradition. He believed that if the village declined the state would decline, and stated that Japan is one small village. Such devotion to the specific issue in a specific locality deemed significant for the whole of the nation has served to revitalize the citizens' anti-pollution movement.

As a theorist of the citizens' movement, a nuclear physicist and former member of the 'World Culture' circle during the war, Taketani Mitsuo (1911–) argues with regard to the issue of public safety that even though the number of victims may be only a small proportion of the entire population, they should still receive the closest attention.[83] We cannot justify the argument that the employees of the company producing the pollution and the consumers of the product outnumber the victims. Even when the number of victims is small, these victims constitute the public, from whose point of view public safety must be measured. On questions of safety, we cannot appeal to simple majorities as in a parliamentary election.

The most famous incident in the anti-pollution movement is the protest against Minamata disease.[84] In 1953, citizens of Minamata City in Kumamoto Prefecture began to suffer from a strange paralytic disease. The disease also affected animals, and cats were seen to dance like rats and die. Between 1953 and 1961, 87 cases were confirmed. Among these there were 37 confirmed deaths.

In 1959, the Welfare Department disclosed that the cause of the disease was mercury poured into the bay from the factory of the Japan Chisso Company. A small group of people rallied around the victims and began a protest against the company and the government. They sued the company and the government and gained a partial victory after many years, bringing the disastrous pollution to public attention. They demonstrated to the public what unauthorized amateurs could achieve on the basis of the hard facts of personal disaster.

The Japanese citizens' movement springs from the village tradition of the pre-Meiji period. Even when it is called the 'circle movement', it has, today, little to do with the form of cultural activity which Kurahara Koreto introduced from Soviet Russia and is more closely related to indigenous customs. It is rooted in the same village tradition which produced *renga*, or linked verse, which may be called an art form originally enjoyed by the circle.

One instance of resistance rooted in the village tradition is the Sunagawa farmers' protest against the enlargement of the airfield for the U.S. military base, which lasted from May 1955 to 18 December 1968, when the U.S. finally gave up the plan.[85] Another is the campaign of the Sanrizuka farmers against the installation of the international airport at Narita, near Tokyo, which began in 1966, although in this case the farmers confronted the authority of the Japanese state itself rather than U.S. military policy backed by the Japanese riot squad. Even so, the tenuous property rights guaranteed to farmers by the constitution could be used to fight the dictates of the government.[86]

In general, a circle is a small, voluntary and temporary community, meeting at regular intervals in pursuit of a common interest, such as flower arrangement, *haiku*, movies or reading. It can also be a study group of contemporary history or of a classic like *The Tale of Genji*, which may take several years of close reading. It is no longer the circle of the few years after 1931 and the few years after 1945, a lower sub-group taking orders from the headquarters of the Japan Communist Party. A circle may form around a specific political problem which has affected people badly, as in the case of Minamata disease, and gather the necessary support from doctors, chemists, reporters, lawyers and ordinary citizens. It tenaciously pursues a specific issue and may achieve partial victories solely through its independence of political parties, since it thus has greater appeal for the public at large and can solicit support from a wider sphere.

A small monthly magazine called *Regional Struggle* is published in Kyoto specifically for the interchange of local information.[87] Political activity of this sort usually centres on specific local issues and so cannot easily spread information to Tokyo. This is its weakness as well as its strength.

In the issue of the pollution of tuna meat in 1954, a housewives' reading circle took the lead, and, with the advice of Yasui Kaoru, a professor of international law, initiated a nationwide movement for the prohibition of atomic and hydrogen bombs, which developed into an international movement holding rallies at Hiroshima and Nagasaki for many years. These rallies were disrupted by friction caused by leftist factions tied to different state authorities. Although the movement began as a free and independent circle, it no longer preserves its original character. Since its disruption by political affiliations, it has become exceedingly difficult to regain the original independence it possessed at the outset.[88]

In the case of the protest against Premier Kishi's use of force to bring about the Military Treaty with the U.S.A. in May and June 1960,[89] and of the protest against the Japanese government's co-operation with the U.S. continuation of the Vietnam War from 1965 to 1973,[90] the federation of free circles created a very large movement which even the political parties could not ignore. In both these cases, the small free circles which took the initiative in forming the federation of circles to pursue a specific issue made it plain that the movement was not dominated by any political party, a precaution not taken by the Anti-Bomb Movement.

When a movement is issue-oriented, however, it disappears with the issue: the protest against Kishi subsided with Kishi's banishment and the Anti-Vietnam War Movement subsided with the

36 Beheiren 'French Demonstration' fills Yaesudori Avenue, 23 June 1970

withdrawal of U.S. troops from Vietnam. The protest against Minamata disease will not come to an end as long as the diseased patients live.

The evaporation of a large issue-oriented movement sometimes strikes onlookers as the outcome of unsteadiness and unreliability. Such movements are different in nature from political parties, which struggle to survive in the face of changing times.

The citizens' movements since the 1960s rely upon ordinary citizens, and on this their character depends, even when they incorporate only a fraction of the population. The ordinary citizen is not concerned with politics *per se*, with who is premier, who is elected to parliament, the titles and nature of new laws. Only when he feels his life affected by the political situation, or his life style hampered by it, does he rouse himself from political apathy and voice his political view in public. The citizen's political interest is in contrast to the political interest of the professional activists whose livelihood depends on being politically well-informed.

Of all postwar Japanese cartoons, 'Sazaesan' by Hasegawa Machiko has enjoyed the longest life, from 1946 right up to the present, as well as the greatest popularity in newspapers, paperback books and on television.[91] A survey of residents in six major cities – Yokohama, Nagoya, Kyoto, Osaka, Kōbe and Kitakyūshū – in 1965, showed that this cartoon was the best-liked in every city, and this was certainly the case in Tokyo also, since this was the city in which the *Asahi* newspapers which serialized 'Sazaesan' had the strongest hold. To Japanese between the ages of two and a hundred, Sazaesan is a familiar figure, almost an acquaintance. In the earliest cartoons, Sazaesan was a girl of 20, living with her parents and siblings. Over the following quarter of a century, she has grown about ten years older and is now a housewife with a husband and infant son, still living with her parents and siblings. I have made a comparison of 'Sazaesan' in 1946, one year after Japan's surrender, and in 1970, ten years after the beginning of the prosperity which has changed the life style of Japanese city dwellers. In the content analysis of the 1946 series, recurrent social themes of cartoons are as follows:

Repatriation from overseas (*4 times*)
Occupation army (*4 times*)
Food hunting trips (*4 times*)
Gardening in the family back yard (*3 times*)
Infectious disease (*twice*)

Rationing (*twice*)
Substitute food (*once*)
Lack of fuel (*once*)
Quick course for learning English (*once*)
Unhealthy food products (*once*)
Black market (*once*)
Inflation, in connection with rises in postal stamp prices
   (*once*)
Debate on the equality of rights of men and women (*once*)
Democratization of police (*once*)
War veterans' return (*once*)
War orphans (*once*)
Preparation to ward off typhoon (*once*)
Criticism of teachers (*once*)
Cattle (*once*)

There are 78 independent strips, each consisting of four pictures,
and of these, social themes appear in 33, or 41 per cent. The others
treat ordinary family events.

In 1970, social themes appear in 27 of the 96 stories (29 per
cent). The social themes are:

The Expo (*7 times*)
Inflation (*4 times*)
Hardworking clerks (*3 times*)
Pollution (*twice*)
Old age pension (*once*)
Over-protection of children (*once*)
A bank robbery of Yen 3 billion (*once*)
Disposal of rubbish (*once*)
Position of Japan as economic super power (*once*)
Scarcity of middle-school graduates going directly into
   employment (*once*)
Part-time jobs for housewives (*once*)
High taxes (*once*)
Cheating in professional baseball (*once*)
The contradiction of capitalism (*once*)
Currency crisis (*once*)

Ordinary Citizens and Citizens' Movements

In the years immediately following Japan's surrender, women were forced to leave home in order to procure a livelihood for the Family. They had to be alert to all kinds of information. In the 1960s and 1970s the household was secure. The young housewife no longer needed to leave home and re-examine her social outlook. Most necessary information was brought to the household through television. The only social theme that initially engaged her interest seems to have been inflation, in which Japan led the world, which naturally affected her style of living.

Judging from the circulation of the *Asahi*, in which 'Sazaesan' was serialized, its readership has been 15 million for the past 30 years. Taking into account television viewing, more than 20 million people have access to these cartoons. Thus 'Sazaesan' reflects the social outlook of 15 to 20 million ordinary Japanese.

37–38   From *Sazaesan*, Vol. 46, by Hasegawa Machiko

Frame 1 *(She)* –   We've been asked out. I might wear my kimono.
   (He) –   That's a great idea. There's no femininity in Western clothes these days.

Frame 2 – Now I'm ready!

Their outlook, and 'Sazaesan's' outlook, seems to be:

1. denigration of militarism as something that should not be repeated;
2. satisfaction with the everyday life of the family, from which point of view an excessive craving for better positions, exemplified by hard-working company clerks or children pushed to study, seems funny;
3. a fundamental belief that all men should be equal before the law: the standards required of children must be kept by the father, and boys and girls are to be judged by the same moral criteria. That gives 'Sazaesan' an instant supply of material from the social life of Japan even after Japan had achieved prosperity.

'Sazaesan's' love of comfort may be open to criticism in that it overlooks the economic imperialism of Japan in the 1960s and 1970s, but there are two saving features. There is no trace of prewar ideology which justified dispatching military forces to protect Japan's economic interests; and there is a fundamental faith in the way of life of the ordinary woman, together with a rejection of excessive effort to succeed, including to amass national wealth. All this explains 'Sazaesan's' sympathy with the banishment of Kishi, the Premier responsible for war, in 1960, and with the anti-pollution movement, including the Minamata movement, in the 1970s. Nevertheless, this is not a sympathy with a revolutionary movement.

Members of co-ordination committees of citizens' movements, following Taketani Mitsuo and Kuno Osamu[92] and Nakai Masakazu, whose views I have quoted, aimed for the independent development of citizens' movements, working in collaboration with the Communist and Socialist parties, while reserving their right to criticize these political parties. They never entertained the illusion that the citizens' movement was revolutionary. They emphasized that the revolutionary movement, and also revolutionary government, could learn much from an independent resistance movement. Their point of view was not shared by leftist parties and leaders. Some tried to draw the whole of the citizens' movement into the revolutionary movement. Others seemed to think that their efforts in the citizens' movement were revolutionary, confusing resistance with revolution.[93]

8 Comments on Patterns of Life

Yanagita Kunio wrote the *History of Modern Japan – Changing Signs of the Times* in 1930, using no proper names and basing his history on the evidence of newspapers.[94]

Yanagita was a unique scholar. He was a moderate, who dismissed most of his so-called moderate contemporaries as reactionaries. He thus managed to avoid many of the misjudgements of the prewar radical progressives and reactionaries and also the redirection which radicals, progressives and reactionaries underwent during the Fifteen Years' War. Yanagita was one of the very few who did not lose sight of the cultural continuity between pre-Meiji and post-Meiji Japan. On the whole, Yanagita criticized the post-Meiji government from the point of view of the continuous cultural tradition, or folkways, of the Japanese people. A major challenge facing modern scholars is how to write a sequel to Yanagita's *History* covering the period after 1955.

The defeat of 1945 and the subsequent occupation by the U.S.A. brought about some drastic institutional changes in Japan,[95] although, with the hindsight of 35 years, these changes no longer seem as great as they seemed at the time to the Occupation authorities and many Japanese opinion leaders.[96] In the 1960s and 1970s high economic growth changed the face of Japan. Between 1955 and 1975 a great change took place.[97] Of the total workforce, those engaged in agriculture numbered 41.1 per cent in 1955 and 13.8 per cent in 1975. In January 1979, 12 per cent of Japanese families were agricultural. Agriculture became to a large extent the work of grandmothers and mothers, and commuting to city factories and companies increased.

The crucial question is, how much cultural change occurred in the era of great economic growth?

116

With regard to food, Japanese self-sufficiency has decreased markedly. In terms of grain, it has fallen from 82 per cent in 1960 to 34 per cent in 1978, an alarming drop from the 1977 figure of 40 per cent. In terms of beans, it has fallen from 44 per cent in 1960 to 11 per cent in 1974. For animal meat the figure has dropped from 96 per cent in 1960 to 60 per cent in 1974. Only in terms of rice has Japan's level of self-sufficiency been unchanged, standing at 102 per cent in 1974.[98]

During the Fifteen Years' War, Japan suffered a food shortage, and towards the end of the war people were forced to replace rice with substitutes and were encouraged to eat bread. After the defeat and during the Occupation, imported corn and wheat were introduced into everyday life. Schoolchildren were given skimmed milk and bread. A campaign was initiated, claiming that rice was unhealthy and made one sleepy and sluggish. Some writers claim that this was a conspiracy by the government on behalf of the U.S.A. intended to encourage imports from America. Eating rice is no longer considered unhealthy by specialists in nutrition, and, in fact, cardiologists both in Japan and abroad recommend traditional Japanese cooking with its mixture of unrefined rice, kelp seaweed, vegetables, beans and fish, and consider that with less salt and soya sauce it would be an ideal menu for those over middle age. But since the start of the war and in the following 35 years the ingredients of traditional Japanese cooking have become difficult to procure. The cheap dishes of the Meiji and Taishō Periods are now the most expensive, and a hamburger, frankfurter or croquette, delicacies in the Meiji Period, are now cheap and easily accessible fast foods. In the Edo Period, the three greatest delicacies were silver carp *sushi*, dried mullet roe and sea urchin (sea chestnut), none of which attract young people today, who prefer the food popular in America and Canada.

The Society for the Study of Contemporary Customs, begun in 1976, asked its 500 members in 1978 about their breakfast habits. This we can ascertain only by asking, because our mode of living is undergoing such a swift change in the years of high economic growth. Only 6 per cent of the society's members, mainly middle-class city dwellers whose ages range between 20 and 70, ate a traditional Japanese breakfast of boiled rice, bean-paste soup, fermented soy beans, pickles and Japanese tea.[99] Moreover, the concept of what constitutes the middle class is itself highly vague, now that 90 per cent of Japanese place themselves within it.[100]

39–40   Two types of Japanese breakfast

Engel's coefficient, which indicates the proportion of the household budget spent on food, was over 44 per cent in 1960, and 34 per cent in 1970, comparable to European countries.[101] Parallel with this change, the daily menus of the Japanese now commonly include hamburgers, croquettes, veal cutlets, curry or omelettes with rice. On the other hand, the simple foods which were so easy to procure before the war have become the object of nostalgia. Citizens affected by pollution declared that they would rather eat simple rice balls with pickled plums in clean air than beef steak under a smoke-filled sky. Such a desire has become more and more difficult to satisfy since the 1960s. The anti-pollution movement, which is continued today by a small minority in each locality, is in this sense linked to the wishes of ordinary citizens who do not participate in demonstrations and sit-ins. It is very seldom that direct action by anti-pollution groups is molested or ridiculed by the majority of citizens.

During the early stage of high economic growth, in 1960, the representative financial groups proposed an agricultural policy with two objectives: to mechanize and aggrandize traditional agricultural methods; and to abandon self-sufficiency in agricultural products. The ruling party accepted this proposal and directed labour power from agriculture into industry. With this object in mind, the government drew up the basic agriculture law of 1961. Today the income of agricultural families comes mainly from industry, with about four-fifths being provided by husbands, sons and daughters who work in factories. The small-scale agriculture carried on by grandparents and mothers with the help of expensive machinery is not highly productive, nor is it able to compete with overseas production, particularly that of the U.S.A. With the exception of rice, the price of which is given legal protection, agricultural products have gone down both in quality and quantity. The Conservative Party has benefited agricultural families in two ways, by increasing their income and by raising the price of rice, and so has received their support ever since the land reform during the Occupation.

The farmers' reaction to the basic agricultural law is typified by two incidents. Farmers in Akita Prefecture in northern Japan agreed to the draining of Lake Hachirōgata, the second largest lake in Japan, to provide new land for rice production. When the drainage had been completed, a surplus of rice necessitated a change of policy on the part of the government regarding the distribution of bonus money to farmers for not producing rice. The

119

farmers obeyed the government's order and accepted the loss of a fishing site and play area for their children.[102]

The Hachirōgata farmers, according to the agricultural economist Iinuma Jirō, are the 'teacher's pet' of the Japanese government, and indirectly of the U.S. government. The unruly pupils are the farmers of Sanrizuka, who refused to accept the government's proposal to buy their land for the building of an international airport, in spite of the enormous sums offered them, and continued to cultivate their land. Although their income was small and shrinking further, they could survive on their own produce, and were suspicious that a large amount of cash would not provide them with a healthy way of life.[103]

The government policy of high industrialization at the cost of agriculture has so far made Japan a prosperous country, to the envy of other nations. It has urbanized much of Japan and turned the majority of Japanese into city dwellers. This represents a decisive break with pre-Meiji tradition.[104] Yanagita Kunio says in his *History of Modern Japan – Changing Signs of the Times* that the Japanese are a nation who consider the outdoors as a part of the house. Streets are where adults meet and converse and where children spend most of their waking time playing. This way of life was probably brought from southern islands. But now, shut up in mammoth buildings and living in small partitions, the Japanese have little time to associate with one another, and children little time and space to play. Even young people with time and money are said to tend towards what Nakano Osamu calls 'Capsule Man', who feels most secure and relaxed when he is shut up in his small room with his stereo, television and comic books.[105] They have developed a love and respect for privacy, a distrust of public causes, and have very little regard for the state. A survey of employees of an electrical company showed that not a single one was prepared to give his life for the state in a time of emergency, in decisive contrast to the mentality of the prewar and wartime eras.

Yanagita Kunio quotes from an *Asahi* newspaper of 1929 the story of an old tramp, 95 years old, who carried as his only luggage 45 wooden mortuary name tablets of his deceased ancestors. He would not throw them away for fear the ancestral ghosts would not only hound him but would haunt somebody else and make mischief. That was two years before Japan plunged into a long

**41   High-rise housing estates, Takashimadaira,
Tokyo, 1973**

war. Then the belief still existed that each person should work for
the continuation of his family. The ancestral spirit of the family
would be with the living and give assistance. Such a belief in the
family spirit has dwindled in the postwar period. In more and more
city houses, there is no place for family mortuary tablets. The
anxiety that haunted the 95-year-old wanderer of 1929 no longer
torments the city dwellers of 1980. The transformation is not due
to the Japanese people's conversion to Christianity.

According to Takatori Masao, a scholar of the Japanese folk
religion, the Japanese word for a memento, *katami*, originates in
seeing the missing form. Keeping a memento, then, presupposes
an ability to see the missing form of a person now deceased.
However, this ability, supposedly universal for much of the history
of Japanese culture, has declined swiftly in the years of prosperity
since 1960. The spread of photographs, radio, gramophones, tape
recorders, television and videos has contributed to the deterior-
ation of the ability to conjure up missing forms through a
memento. Today, very few city dwellers keep mementoes of their
ancestors, even grandparents or parents, in their homes.[106] This is
partly due to the smallness of their houses, but a more important
reason is the change of dwelling place: most city dwellers lived
previously in the country, where the natural surroundings them-

selves contained innumerable mementoes which enabled them to conjure up the images of the deceased, thus educating them to see the missing forms of familiar figures.

Changes in dress have also contributed to the decline. With Japanese dress, cloth can be preserved and reused again and again. When one dress is discarded, the cloth is washed and dried, and used as a part of some other dress. In this way, a grandmother's dress may live on as part of her granddaughter's pyjamas. According to Japanese animist tradition, the spirit is transmitted together with the material. The transmission of the material naturally evokes in the mind of the granddaughter the imaginary scene of the grandmother as a child. Until the 1920s, most Japanese wore traditional dress. After 1931, the war encouraged efficiency and, in spite of the traditionalist ideology of the wartime government, accelerated a thorough Westernization in the dress of men and women at work and also at school, although both men and women continued to wear traditional Japanese clothing at home for a long time after the war. Since the 1960s, the majority of Japanese men and women have worn Western clothes even at home.[107] According to a survey made from 24-hour TV recordings of city dwellers in big flats, men spend their waking hours at home in underwear, children in pyjamas, and wives in simple Western dress.[108] When such a mode of life is adopted, there is no room left for the transmission of an ancestral family spirit in the form of clothing.

There remains, however, a vague sense of ancestor worship which envelops the nation. This unity is symbolized by the person of the Emperor. In this sense, at least, the Emperor has not been outgrown. The Emperor is a symbol of the self-containment of the Japanese people. Thus, unless there is another war and defeat that brings about its downfall through a foreign agency, the emperor system will not become obsolete until the condition of self-containment undergoes a radical change. This change is, I believe, taking place, but it is a gradual one.

The solidarity of the Japanese as a nation is still very strong, as indicated by their constant use of the word 'foreigner', and will continue to be so for a very long time. This mentality contributed to Japan's swift recovery from the devastation brought about by the war, and to the vigorous atmosphere of private enterprise in

Japan. The historian of technology, Hoshino Yoshirō, has characterized postwar technology in Japan in terms of the ability to be excited about minor technical innovations. In Europe and North America, inventive engineers are interested only in innovations of radical novelty. In Japan, however, engineers are excited over minor innovations often brought from abroad, and the excitement is instantly shared by the group.[109] Japanese enterprise makes money from these minor innovations, and the success of Japanese technology has invited the jealousy of the U.S.A., which responds by forcing Japan to buy more agricultural produce and thus brings about a further decline in self-sufficiency.

High industrialization has made pollution a problem that will haunt Japan for many years. In every region there has sprung up a local group that opposes pollution. There has arisen a romantic longing for a simple life with the recycling of waste products, a limited use of mechanical means and energy, a return to traditional food and housing and, in sum, a lower standard of living. At what point we check our reliance upon technology in our own individual life style and also in our national life style is the question now facing Japan, and which will determine our future.

Some clues lie in the actions of the Japanese in the 35 years following the surrender. In 1947, right after the war, the birth rate per 10,000 was 34.3. It was 33.5 in 1948, 33.0 in 1958, sank to 17.2 in 1962 and 13.88 in 1966. According to the estimate disclosed by the Population Institute in 1979, the Japanese population has stabilized, and will reach zero population growth after 50 years, remaining at 139 million.[110] Population is a major factor in the intellectual and cultural history of a nation. To check population growth was an intellectual achievement of the Japanese nation, which will encourage it to deviate from the course followed since the Meiji Period.[111] Population growth was often used as a pretext for Japan's military expansion in the prewar years. It takes a certain growth in national self-esteem to have brought about such a check upon the size of population. This growth in self-esteem, coupled with the abandonment of the prewar concept of the national structure, exercises a check on the re-emergence of the ideology of militarist expansion in the era of high economic growth.

There have been proposals for a renewal of military conscription, for nuclear armament, and for the revision of the constitution by which Japan has given up the right to wage war, but so far they have not met with popular support. This self-esteem, which we might call postwar egoism, in combination with the collapse of the national myth of the infallibility of the Emperor, will for quite some time serve as a negative guideline for the Japanese people in making decisions on national and diplomatic policies. In spite of the fact that they remain under the nuclear umbrella of the U.S.A., this self-regard and the distrust of the national myth will incline the Japanese people not to yield to the pressure of the U.S.A.

In 1979, there was a controversy between two economists, Morishima Michio and Seki Yoshihiko.[112] Seki, who had held a liberal viewpoint throughout the war years and had been a critic of militarism all through, supported open armament for Japan in the postwar years. Morishima, on the other hand, argued that in the event of invasion by an outside power the Japanese should resort to organized surrender. He claims that this would cause the least damage to the Japanese people. Although Seki's argument is tinged with the sincere moral fervour worthy of a liberal of the war years, Morishima's proposal seems to be more in agreement with the life style of the Japanese people since the 1960s.

9 A Comment on Guidebooks on Japan

When we arrived in Montreal in 1979, my son began to attend a high school, where he was given a textbook on history called *The Story of Modern Nations*, written in 1958 and used for the ninth and tenth grades. The textbook included a chapter on Japan, which contained the following summary of Japanese cultural history:

> Japan has no great literature. No one has dared to write anything that might offend the upper classes. The literature of Japan has always followed fixed forms, just as the lives of the people themselves have been regulated by their rulers. The poetry of the Japanese shows their rigid observance of rules and patterns, as well as the love of making small, dainty things. The forms came originally from China and have been much the same for a thousand years. Almost the only poems are the *tanka*, a five-line poem of only thirty-one syllables, and an even smaller poem, the *hokku* (hok'koo), in three lines with only seventeen syllables. Often the poet describes only a small detail of a scene or a mood, but if he is accomplished he may suggest much more by these details. Japanese women excel in these small poems, in which each word is the 'leaf of an idea' which is supposed to suggest more than the word itself.[113]

The textbook goes on to make several other assertions about Japan which were factually wrong even in 1958. The above summary would be insufficient to explain *The Tale of Genji* by Lady Murasaki of the Heian Period, a work unparalleled in

Chinese or European literature, and the egalitarian social thought
of Andō Shōeki in the middle of the Edo Period, whose work was
highly esteemed by E. H. Norman, a Canadian historian, and
which preceded that of J. J. Rousseau.

These factual inadequacies aside, the comparative perspective
of the book seems to me to be useful. It could have gone further
and described Japan's hasty imitation of Commodore Perry's
forcible opening of the country in the relationship with Korea in
the early Meiji Period. The imitation has been carried out in such a
variety of ways that Japan serves as a useful mirror for Western
civilization itself. In the prosperity of the sixties and seventies,
Japanese enterprise successfully adapted Western technological
innovations in such a way that they profited more than the
countries of their origin. At the same time, Japan discarded the
dual wage structure that characterized the Japanese economy up
to the 1960s. Group cohesiveness arising out of self-containment
contributed to Japan's success in the competition with the industry
of other developed nations.

A different interpretation may be made of this cultural trend. A
Mexican anthropologist, Ricardo d'Amare, tells of a Swedish
engineer whose faith in Europe was shattered by what he saw on
his trip to Japan. He had been raised in the belief that European
civilization was like a magnificent tapestry, science and art
embedded in love and a religious upbringing. In Japan he found
odd techniques and beliefs of obviously European lineage combined piecemeal and functioning efficiently at a low cost. The
people did not seem versed in the humanistic culture of Europe,
but they none the less accomplished time-saving jobs in a way that
was expedient enough. This Swedish engineer succumbed to a
nervous breakdown. Perhaps he was an unusually susceptible
character, but even so his story exemplifies a way of looking at
Japanese culture which is humiliating to Europeans, and in being
humiliating it teaches them something.

In mid-February 1978, a test was given to 61 sixth-formers in
Hertfordshire in England as a prelude to a one-day conference on
Japan. A clear majority agreed that religion still dominates the
daily life of most Japanese, a claim which is hard to reconcile with
the many surveys which reveal the Japanese as one of the most
avowedly agnostic peoples in the world (which will, in my opinion,

42 Illustrations from a guidebook on Japan, showing the Japanese love of bathing and the custom of exchanging gifts

necessitate re-examination of the concept of religion in contemporary society). Twenty-five students believed that Japanese export success was based on the low wages paid to Japanese workers. In fact, the wages of Japanese industrial workers surpassed those of their British counterparts by about 1968–1970. Regarding Japan's problems there was substantial agreement, with over-population coming top of the list (20), followed by lack of resources (11) and lack of land (8). Only four students named pollution. The test revealed a good deal of confusion between Japan and pre-modern China, as the children expected to see rickshaws, sampans and bound feet in contemporary Japan. Although the British children described scattered images of both

43   An image of the Japanese as portrayed by the Malaysian cartoonist Lat

industrialized and pre-industrial Japan, they did see the disjunction between the view of Japan as a traditional, poor, backward country and of Japan as a provider of modern industrial goods. They saw a need to emphasize that such products can only be manufactured by skilled and educated workers. Such implications aside, these children hit upon the main problem in understanding modern Japanese culture – that is, to recognize the disjunction between highly industrialized culture and traditional culture and to look for some plausible explanation.

The misconceptions of British schoolchildren regarding Japan are often duplicated in Western guidebooks. *The Japan Handbook* by Richard Tames,[114] from which I have just quoted these former examples of the English conception of Japan, begins with ignorance and proceeds by further examining this ignorance, a variant of the Socratic method. Most of the misleading guidebooks to Japan give either a one-sided picture of traditional Japanese culture or a factually false account of the merging of the traditional and the industrial sides. *Tokyo* (Mitsuaki Usami and Cheung Hong-Chung, 1978),[115] for instance, gives a colourful picture of the star festival of 7 July, and of streets full of people in traditional dress for the summer Nebuta Festival. It represents Tokyo as a festival city. In fact only a very small percentage of Tokyo's citizens are descendants of residents of the old city, Edo, and most of the inhabitants of Tokyo have no connection with the local festivals today. The city is characterized by its uprootedness. The colourful festival photographed in this guidebook is a commercial embellishment of one of the shopping centres. The Nebuta Festival march is actually a local custom of northern Japan and in Tokyo is a commercial advertisement. Thus *Tokyo* does not provide a true picture of Tokyo life. The picture is tailored to suit the preconceived ideas of overseas tourists and to offer what they would like to see in Tokyo. It might be classed as a product of exoticism.

Products of exoticism spring also from the Japanese themselves. *The Postwar Period in Literature* (1979),[116] a book of conversations between Ayukawa Nobuo and Yoshimoto Takaaki, the two foremost poets in postwar Japan, refers to the last stage of the literary output of Mishima Yukio. Yoshimoto speaks of Mishima as a writer of genius who succumbed in his last years to the temptation of exporting to the world literature market. Japanese culture offers a readily exportable product in the cult of the samurai which culminated in *kamikaze* attacks and *harakiri*. Katō Shūichi, a critic radically opposed to Yoshimoto, says in *The Age of Transformation* (1979)[117] that the Buddhism depicted in the last of Mishima's novels, the *Sea of Fertility*, is a Buddhism designed for tourists from overseas. It has little relation to the Buddhism that has been part of Japanese life for 1,500 years. The exoticism of Mishima's later works explains his popularity in Europe and North America.

Inadequate guidebooks try to satisfy the preconceived ideas of tourists instead of refuting them. More adequate guidebooks try to draw tourists' attention towards the people of the country who do not speak the language in which the guidebook is written, an approach seldom taken even by the Japanologists of super states such as the Soviet Union and the U.S.A. To take a metaphor from the performing arts, in the harmonious dialogue between the guest god and the local god, it is more important to decipher the silent grimace and halting speech of the local god than the fluent, universalistic statement of the guest god. One can attempt to decipher the silence and faltering speech without attaining a mastery of Japanese. Even with an adequate knowledge of the Japanese language, one may fail to decipher the clues given in this faltering speech, if one is satisfied with the preconceived ideas of a universalization already achieved.

Where there is a disjunction between industrialization and tradition, there are many issues on which the guest god and the local god are engaged in dialogue. The guest god may not necessarily stand for industrialization and the local god may not necessarily stand for traditional culture. Although the central government has tended to promote industrialization, there have also been attempts to take over traditional culture and to change it into the form acceptable to the ruling elite and also to guests from the super powers.

Of the many issues, I will point to three which inadequate guidebooks tend to overlook. One is the disjunction between pollution and *The Book of Seasons*. Pollution is one of the gravest problems of which Japanese are conscious today. That comes naturally from the fact that Japan is a heavily industrialized, small island country. Most citizens are sympathetic to the anti-pollution movement, whether or not they actively participate. In the mind of contemporary Japanese there remains a picture of a time when the seasons could be enjoyed. This is the ideal of *The Book of Seasons*, compiled by Takizawa Bakin (1767–1848) in the late Edo Period, which gave guidelines for the composition of 17-syllable poems on various seasonal subjects.[118] It is a calendar compiled in the form of an aesthetic dictionary, which classifies the subjects of poetry since the Nara Period. The use of seasonal subjects in poetry has existed since these early times, and became widely

130

popular even among the lower classes in the Edo Period. *The Book of Seasons* thus represents a cult of the common man in that any man with a rudimentary knowledge of the Japanese language can produce a poem by following its guidelines. It is a way of enjoying what each season brings, an ideal which has taken on a new meaning in the era of pollution since the 1960s.

War and religion together form a second neglected problem. The image of war in the past and in the future is closely tied to the religious consciousness of the Japanese. Up to 1945, war meant victory and profit to the Japanese. Since then, it has meant hardship, humiliation and loss, although overseas wars such as the Korean and Vietnam wars have brought profit to Japan. The problem of how to avert another war involving the Japanese has been a part of the social consciousness of the common citizen even in the current era of prosperity. The revision of the present constitution in order to restore the right to wage war has never gained popular support. The spectacular ten-year growth of the Sōkagakkai from one remaining believer, Toda Jōsei, to more than one million and a position as the third political force in parliament in 1980 may be attributed to the death of its leader Makiguchi Tsunesaburō in prison during the war. There has been a movement toward the resurrection of state Shinto which has provided the ideological basis for the military expansion of Japan since the Meiji era. The progress of this movement in the near future will be a touchstone to the development of Japanese religious consciousness, which has centred on the preservation of the memory of war.

These two issues suggest that a fruitful project for the 1980s[119] would be a re-examination of the Edo Period, an era of zero growth, and of how the norms of that period could be reformulated in conditions of growth.

There are problems that cannot be subsumed under that heading. In the Tames guidebook, British children note that Japan is a country where people speak the Japanese language. This is an insight into the cultural trait which I call self-containment. The defeat of 1945 and subsequent occupation made the Japanese conscious, for the first time in their history, of a third problem, the non-Japanese living in their country. The importance of the literature written in the Japanese language by Koreans resident in

Japan gained unprecedented recognition in postwar Japan.[120] The Japanese became conscious of the social discrimination suffered by the 60,000 Koreans living in Japan, and of the value of maintaining the postwar declaration of non-belligerency. Their presence has made us conscious of the value of our constitution. The issues which arise from this problem elude the eye of the super state and of Japanologists bred in the ideology of such a super state.[121]

The relationship between the Japanese and the cultures of other countries has posed problems which were considered some time ago. How to apply *The Book of Seasons* to life in occupied territories in the South Sea islands was a matter of controversy among the *haiku* poets of the war years. Nagata Hidejirō (1876–1943), formerly Mayor of Tokyo and Minister of Communication, argued that each place in the world has its own book of seasons.[122] Since he was an important adviser to the military administration of Singapore, his opinion obviously carried political weight. In 1918 the nationalist Ashizu Kōjirō strongly protested against the erection in Korea of a Shinto shrine with the founding goddess of Japan (Amaterasu Ōmikami) as the object of worship.[123] He wrote, in an open letter to the government, that the Japanese Shinto tradition was to venerate the gods of each locality, and that a shrine built in Korea should therefore be dedicated to the gods of Korea. This, he argued, was the Japanese way. This way of thinking which was part of orthodox Japanese tradition, was not favoured by those in power in the prewar and war years, but was afforded new value in the 1960s. One of the main problems of the age of prosperity is to check the formless development of our national life. *The Book of Seasons*, with its cult of the common man, offers an ideal of the simple life which we must seek anew in the future post-growth period. In the meantime, we will seek, through various forms of greed and self-esteem, a more natural safeguard against the resurrection of militarism which seems to be favoured by the super state. Contemporary comic books, songs and Great River Dramas on television offer various signs of greed and self-regard. We must develop an adequate and reliable inconography to decipher these signs. On this topic also, most guidebooks and Japanologists in the U.S.A. and the Soviet Union are silent.

In respect to literature, the writers – such as Ibuse Masuji and

Nakano Shigeharu who are important in the Japanese context but regarded as a insignificant in Europe – should be paid more attention.[124]

References

1 Occupation: the American Way of Life as an Imposed Model

1 A controversy arose in 1978 between Etō Jun and Honda Shūgo concerning 'unconditional' versus 'conditional' surrender and was argued out in the dailies *Mainichi Shinbun* and *Asahi Shinbun*, the weekly *Asahi Journal*, the monthly literary journal *Bungei*, and the weekly book review paper *Shūkan Dokushojin*. Etō was taking issue with the assumption behind the phrase, 'as a result of Japan's unconditional surrender', used by Hirano Ken in his *Shōwa Bungakushi* (A History of Literature in the Showa Period), Chikuma Shobō, 1963; he claimed that this assumption was an underlying cause of the bankruptcy of postwar Japanese literature.

Honda wrote 'On the meaning of "unconditional surrender"' (*Bungei*, September 1978), taking on the mantle of the late Hirano Ken, one of his fellow editors of the magazine *Kindai Bungaku* (Modern Literature). This article formed the starting point of the Honda versus Etō controversy. Etō's arguments can be found in two books: *Wasureta Koto to Wasuresaserareta Koto* (Things We Have Forgotten and Things We Have Been Forced to Forget), Bungei Shunjūsha, 1979, and *Mō Hitotsu no Sengoshi* (An Alternative Postwar History), Kōdansha, 1978.

This controversy remained to the end a conflict where the many participants on both sides conceded nothing. This was partly because of the confusion between the aspect of ascertaining the facts, and the ideological aspect of interpreting those facts; and also because each party sought a single meaning corresponding to every term.

First of all, the Potsdam Declaration of 1945 stated the conditions of peace with Japan, so in this sense, the peace was conditional. (On this point, Etō was confirming what had already been stated by legal experts Taoka Ryōichi and Takano Yūichi.) The Potsdam Declaration also demanded the 'unconditional surrender of all the Japanese Armed Forces'. The postwar Japanese media (as well as Ministry of Foreign Affairs documents) reduced to 'unconditional surrender' the legal fact that Japan had accepted the *unconditional surrender* of the armed forces in an *unconditional way* that allowed for no bargaining. This abridged term gained wide currency in postwar Japan. A look at postwar monthly magazines shows that the use of the term 'unconditional surrender' is taken for granted. The establishment of such a term reflects the wishes of the Occupation forces who controlled the Japanese mass media and did

134

References

not allow any challenge to their decisions. One could say that this attitude
of the Occupation forces deviated from a straight interpretation of the
Potsdam Declaration, but the psychosocial reality of 'unconditional
surrender', including this approach of the Occupation forces, continued
for some time after 1945.

The position which tries to reverse this way of thinking by returning to
the Potsdam Declaration on which it is based, is also a possibility.
Following Taoka Ryōichi and Takano Yūichi, Inoue Kiyoshi and Suzuki
Masashi's *Nihon Kindaishi* (Modern History of Japan), Gōdō Shup-
pansha, 1956, takes the theory of conditional surrender from the left-wing
viewpoint, the exact opposite of Etō's stance. The same line is followed in
Mimura Fumio's 'Potsudamu sengen judaku wa mujōken kōfuku de atta
ka – sengoshi saidai no mujun ni tsuite' (Was the acceptance of the
Potsdam Declaration an unconditional surrender? – the biggest contradic-
tion of postwar history), *Rekishi Hyōron*, April 1965, and in Inoue
Kiyoshi's 'Sengo Nihon no rekishi' (The history of postwar Japan), in
Gendai no Me, August 1965.

Etō's conditional surrender argument differed from the opinions of
these predecessors and represented a denial of the interpretation of
contemporary history by the so-called postwar progressives; so in
combination with the change in *Zeitgeist*, it had considerable influence.

Isoda Kōichi's *Sengoshi no Kūkan* (The Space of Postwar History)
Shinchōsha, 1983, is a scrupulous record following the oscillations of the
term 'unconditional surrender', distinguishing four phases: 1945, the early
Occupation, post-Occupation, and post-1960s, which saw the recovery of
confidence by the Japanese ruling class.

Fujimura Michio's *Futatsu no senryō to Shōwashi* (Two occupations and
a history of the Shōwa Period) in *Sekai*, August 1981, places two
occupations in a time span of half a century, the first occurring in 1931
when a petty officer of the Japanese Army caused the 'Manchurian
Incident', and the 'semi-occupation' of Japan by the military, and the
second being the 'Occupation' of Japan by the American forces after the
defeat in 1945. According to this view, the war which began with the
invasion of China in 1931 was a 40-year war which lasted until the
restoration of diplomatic relations between Japan and China in 1972:

The Fifteen Years' War view of history which directly links the
Manchurian Incident (1931) with Pearl Harbour, and the theory of
fascism and the Emperor System which goes with the historical
view, denied the dynamism of history by underestimating the
possibilities which existed for preventing the war between the
Manchurian Incident and the Marco Polo Bridge Incident (1937).
As a result, postwar democracy was unable to correctly grasp the
historical significance of the early Shōwa period movement to
protect parliamentary democracy, and was not fully able to inherit
the prewar democratic tradition in Japan. The Fifteen Years' War
theory needs to be re-examined in conforming to historical reality.

A Cultural History of Postwar Japan

This criticism by Fujimura Michio presents a major point of contention for future research in Shōwa history.

2 Baerwald, Hans H., *The Purge of Japanese Leaders under the Occupation*, University of California Press, 1959 (Japanese translation by Sodei Rinjirō, published as *Shidōsha Tsuihō*, Keisei Shobō, 1970).

3 Since then, detailed records pertaining to war responsibility have been compiled by Yamanaka Hisashi, Takasaki Ryūji and Sakuramoto Tomio:

Yamanaka Hisashi, *Bokura Shōkokumin* (We, the Junior Patriots), Henkyōsha, 1974.
Mitami Ware (Your Faithful Servant), Henkyōsha, 1975.
Uchiteshi Yamamu (Fight to the Death), Henkyōsha, 1977.
Hoshigarimasen, Katsu Made wa (I shall want nothing, until victory), Henkyōsha, 1979.
Shōri no Hi Made (Until the Day of Victory), Henkyōsha, 1980.
Shōkokumin Taiken o Saguru (In Search of the Junior Patriot Experience), Henkyōsha, 1981.
Shōkokumin Nōto (Notes on the Junior Patriots), Henkyōsha, 1982.
Shiryō: Senji Shōkokumin no Uta (Documents: Wartime Songs of the Junior Patriots), Nippon Columbia Records. (Gzt 101–2), 1978. Because of harassment only 1,000 copies were released.
Senchū Kyōiku no Uramado (The Back Window of Wartime Education), Asahi Shinbunsha, 1979.
Takasaki Ryūji, *Sensō Bungaku Tsūshin* (War Literature Newsletter), Fūbaisha, 1975.
Senjika no Zasshi – sono Hikari to Kage (The Light and Dark Sides of Wartime Magazines), Fūbaisha, 1976.
Senjika Bungaku no Shūhen (The Periphery of Wartime Literature), Fūbaisha, 1981.
Sakuramoto Tomio, *Hinomaru wa Mite Ita* (The Japanese Flag Was Watching), Marujusha, 1982.
Shōkokumin wa Wasurenai (The Junior Patriots Will Not Forget), Marujusha, 1982.
Kūhaku to Sekinin (Void and Responsibility), Miraisha, 1983.
Konno Toshihiko and Sakuramoto Tomio, *Sabetsu Sensō Sekinin Nōto* (Notes on Discrimination and War Responsibility), Yachiyo Shuppan, 1983.

The importance of these publications lies in the fact that they were achieved by the individual efforts of their respective authors. The nation got by with drawing a veil over wartime responsibility. Members of political parties and professional literary circles avoided criticism of those they associated with publicly as fellow members of such groups. For this reason isolated individuals took on the task of collecting records of wartime speech and actions. This is the actual state of postwar Japanese cultural history, whether we are talking about popular or highbrow culture.

136

References

The documents reproduced by Yamanaka, Takahashi and Sakuramoto are reliable; the fact of the very existence of these documents must surely be acknowledged. Interpretation and evaluation of their work must eventually be carried out, but a tendency to avoid fact-finding and move straight on towards the evaluation of poets, writers, philosophers and academics has still not been reversed.

For an index of basic materials available, the following can be listed:

> Fukushima Chūrō and Ōkubo Hisao (eds.), *Dai Tō-a Sensō Shōshi* (Bibliography of the Greater East Asian War) (3 vols.), Nichigai Associates, 1981.
> *Senjika no Genron* (Wartime Public Opinion) (2 vols.), Nichigai Associates, 1982.

4 Matsuura Sōzō, *Senryoka no Genron Dan'atsu* (Suppression of Speech under the Occupation), Gendai Jānarizumu Shuppankai, 1969; Urada Minoru, *Senryōgun no Yūbin Ken'etsu to Yūshu* (The Occupation Army's Mail Censorship and Philately), Nippon Yūshu Shuppan, 1982; Etō Jun, *Wasureta Koto to Wasuresaserareta Koto* (Things We Have Forgotten and Things We Have Been Forced to Forget), Bungei Shunjūsha, 1979.

5 Uchimura Sukeyuki, *Keyūnaru Ryōjoku Satsujinjiken no Seishin Kantei Kiroku* (A Record of Verdicts with Mitigating Factors on an Unusual Sex Murder Case), Sōgensha, 1952; *Kodaira jiken* (The Kodaira Incident), in Uchimura Sukeyuki and Yoshimasu Nobuo, *Nihon no Seishinkantei* (Japanese Verdicts with Mitigating Circumstances), Misuzu Shobō, 1973.

6 Hogben, Lancelot, *From Cave Painting to Comic Strip*, 1949. Japanese translation, Iwanami Bunko, 1979.

2 Occupation: on the Sense of Justice

7 Redfield, Robert, *The Litle Community*, University of Chicago Press, 1955.

8 Ministry of Foreign Affairs (ed.), *Shūsenshiroku* (Historical Record of the End of the War), Shinbun Gekkansha, 1952.

9 Asahi Shinbunsha Legal Reporters (eds.), *Tokyo Saiban* (The Tokyo Trials) (3 vols.), Tokyo Saiban Kankō-kai, 1962.

10 Keenan, Joseph Barry, and Brown, Brendan Francis, *Crimes against International Law*, Washington, D.C., Public Affairs Press, 1950.

11 Maruyama Masao, 'Gunkoku shihaisha no seishinkeitai' (Psychological types of leaders of military states), in *Gendai Seiji no Shisō to Kōdō* (Philosophy and Practice of Modern Politics), Miraisha, 1964.

12 Satō Ryōichi, *Gyakutai no Kiroku* (Records of Atrocity), Ushio Shobō, 1953; Sugamo Prison Legal Affairs Committee, *Harukanaru Minami Jūjisei – Senpan no Jissō* (The Distant Southern Cross – the True Face of War Criminals), Sannō Shobō, 1967. Shiojiri Kimiaki's *Aru Isho ni tsuite* (Concerning a Certain Will), Shakai Shisō Kenkyūkai Shup-

137

panbu, 1951, was published during the Occupation and testified to the unfairness of the trials of B and C grade war criminals. Published later were:

> Utsumi Aiko, *Chōsenjin B C kyū Senpan no Kiroku* (Record of B and C grade Korean War Criminals), Keisō Shobō, 1982.
> Kamisaka Fuyuko, *Sugamo Purizun Jūsangō Teppi* (Iron Door Number Thirteen, Sugamo Prison), Shinchōsha, 1981.
> *Nokosareta Tsuma* (The Wives who were Left Behind), Chūō Kōronsha, 1983.

13 Sugamo Isho Hensankai, *Seiki no Isho* (Wills of the Century), Sugamo Isho Hensankai Kankō Jimusho, 1953.

14 The classification which I carried out can be found in Tsurumi Shunsuke *et al.*, *Atarashii Kaikoku* (Second Opening of the Country); Vol. I of *Nihon no Hyakunen* (Japan's Hundred Years), Chikuma Shobō, 1961; Tsurumi Kazuko, *Social Change and the Individual*, Princeton University Press, 1970.

15 Sakuta Keiichi, 'Shi to no wakai' (Reconciliation with death), in *Ningen Keisei no Shakaigaku* (Sociology of Character Formation), *Gendai Shakaigaku Kōza*, Vol. 5, Yūhikaku, 1964. Reprinted in *Haji no Bunka Saikō* (A Reassessment of the Culture of Shame), Chikuma Shobō, 1967.

16 It would certainly have been rare for such an opinion to be expressed so clearly to the media. Rather than the direct influence of Occupation army censorship, it can be interpreted as self-regulation coming from the awareness of being under occupation, which existed widely among the Japanese.

17 'Seven Heads – to the seven war criminals, including Tōjō Hideki, who were sentenced to death by hanging', Tsuboi Shigeharu:

> Seven heads
> soon
> will hang
>
> For the seven heads
> we will not shed tears
> not because we do not know sorrow
> but because we know
> the tears the People shed
> are so salty
>
> If we could
> put the noose around the seven necks
> with our own hands
> the dead would rise up from their graves
> such deep sorrow
> the people have been made to taste

You who feel sorrow
for those seven heads soon to hang
weep your fill
till your bag of tears bursts
we will not forbid it
as we were once forbidden
to shed tears for sorrow

That is not all
we will
give black necklaces
as a last gift for the seven necks
so that they can cease to breathe
with certainty

Iron guillotine
you
were not prepared
for revolutionaries only
the seven necks soon to be hanged
will give you greeting
which you should accept
mercilessly

Tsuboi Shigeharu wrote two poems using the metaphor of a kettle made from the superlative iron of the Nanbu region (Iwate Prefecture). One, 'To an Iron Kettle', was written during the war, and praised the great war efforts of the people; the other, 'Song of the Iron Kettle', written after the war, extolled the struggle of the people in the society restored to peace. This continuity was pointed out ironically by Yoshimoto Takaaki in his article 'Poets of Yesterday' in *Shigaku*, November 1955.

Tsuboi's 'Seven Heads', which was written immediately on hearing the verdict of the Tokyo Trials on 11 November 1946 reveals the attitude of the Communist Party that even a person who had written poems in praise of the war, and might thereby have sent an indefinite number of young people to their death, if he returns to the Party after the war, will be given the right to look down on the war leaders in this way.

18 Pal's dissenting opinion was first translated into Japanese as *Nihon Muzairon* (Japan Not Guilty), Nihon Shobō, 1952. The title gives the impression that Pal condoned the Japanese war, and was received by the Japanese in this mistaken way. In this, it is quite similar to the Japanese reception earlier of Gandhi, Tagore and Lu Hsun, praising their criticism of British imperialism while overlooking their criticism of Japanese imperialism. Pal's view was more accurately presented later in Tokyo Saiban Kenkyūkai, *Kyōdō Kenkyū Paaru Hanketsusho (A Joint Study of Pal's Judgement)*, Tokyo Saiban Kankōkai, 1966.

19 Looking at the shifts in attitude to altering Article 9 of the constitution, which renounces war, at the end of the Occupation in 1952,

revisionists were in the majority; by 1955 this trend had been reversed; and since 1970 the anti-revisionists have outstripped the revisionists. NHK Hōsō Yoron Chōsajo (ed.), *Zusetsu Sengo Yoronshi* (Illustrated History of Postwar Public Opinion), Nippon Hōsō Shuppan Kyōkai, 1975.

Nishihira Shigeyoshi and others from the Mathematical Statistics Research Institute have conducted public opinion polls under the title *Nihonjin no Kokuminsei* (The Japanese National Character) every five years on six occasions since 1953. The most recently published results are of the poll conducted in 1978, published as *The Japanese National Character: Four*, Idemitsu Shoten, 1982.

'In the Mathematical Statistics Research Institute's 'Japanese National Character' polls, held every five years since 1953, respondents were asked which of the following three opinions they agreed with:
1. Japan as a whole will improve only when the individual achieves happiness.
2. The individual will not achieve happiness until Japan has improved.
3. The good of the country and the happiness of the individual are one and the same thing.

The first opinion which favours the individual remained steady between 25% and 30%, with no great fluctuations. The second statement which favours the nation, fell from 37% to 27%, showing a clearly declining trend, while the third opinion, which views both individual and nation as inseparable, increased from 31% to 41%. In other words, the opinion which puts the nation first, equating national prosperity with individual happiness, has decreased, but the view which emphasizes the individual has not increased: only the view which equates the nation and individual happiness has increased.

In 1978 respondents were asked more precisely to which opinion of the following they felt more inclined:
1. Even if the country prospers, only one section of people profits, and each individual citizen's life will not improve.
2. If the country prospers, each individual citizen's life will improve.

The result was 37% versus 57%. However in a 1971 opinion poll of the Mainichi Shinbun, a mere 18% agreed with the statement, 'The national interest and the interest of the individual are more or less in agreement', with 75% denying it. Therefore, this probably means that increasing the national interest does not directly bear on individual happiness but that individual happiness is unthinkable without national prosperity.' Nishihira Shigeyoshi, *Nihonjin ni totte no kokka – yoron chōsa kara mita* (How the Japanese view the Nation State – as seen in public opinion polls) in *Shisō no Kagaku*, June 1982. This essay was written as part of Nishihira's yet unpublished *Yoron chōsa ni miru Dōjidaishi* (Contemporary History as Seen in the Opinion Polls).

Opinion polls have shown since 1955 that a majority has supported the anti-war Article 9 of the constitution, and that, parallel with this, a majority has also accepted the existence of the Self Defence Corps. This fact may be seen against the background of the view of the nation state indicated by Nishihira. As Maruyama Masao states in *Kenpō Daikyūjō o meguru jakkan no kōsatsu* (A few thoughts concerning Article Nine of the Constitution), in *Kōei no Ichi kara* (From the Position of the Rearguard), Miraisha, 1982, it is possible to interpret Article Nine and the Preface to the Constitution as existing in order to define the direction of the Self Defence Corps, the fact of whose existence cannot actually be denied. It is difficult to predict with any certainty whether this direction will continue to be kept open, but at least it can be said that the Japanese at present possess such a set of values, however fluid.

20 Hayashi Fusao, *Dai Tō-a Sensō Kōteiron* (In Support of the Greater East Asian War), Banchō Shobō, 1964; *Zoku: Dai Tō-a Sensō Kōteiron* (In Support of the Greater East Asian War: a Sequel), Banchō Shobō, 1965.

Hayashi Fusao's writings originally appeared in serial form in Chūō Kōron, parallel with Ueyama Shunpei's *Dai Tō-a Sensō no Imi* (The Meaning of the Greater East Asian War), Chūō Kōronsha, 1964, which was also included in *Dai Tō-a Sensō no Isan* (The Legacy of the Greater East Asian War), Chūkō Sōsho, 1972. In his wish to be free from the Occupation army's view of the Greater East Asian War, he is in the same mould as Hayashi's works. Ueyama's argument, however, inclines towards fixing his gaze on the original sin of the nation state, Japan included, to prevent another eruption of the power structure of the nation state.

21 On 8 April 1982, a decision was brought in the Supreme Court concerning the second appeal in the textbook authorization case (first lodged in 1967). The verdict ordered a return to the Tokyo High Court, with the result that the appeal was continued. Subsequently, a third appeal was lodged in January 1984.

Several more problems arose with textbook authorization. The previous year pressure had been brought to bear to delete the picture by Maruki Iri and his wife Toshi from the senior high school textbook *Gendai Shakai* (Contemporary Society). Following on this, in 1984, cuts were required in a Grade Six primary school textbook. On 5 July 1982, both the *Okinawan Times* and the *Ryūkyū Shinbun* protested against the authorization by Monbushō of cuts from Japanese history textbooks of atrocities committed against the citizens of Okinawa by Japanese troops in the Battle of Okinawa.

On 26 July 1982, the Chinese Foreign Ministry protested against the replacing in Japanese history textbooks of the word 'invasion' of China with the vaguer 'advance'. South Korean, Thai and Hong Kong newspapers all published protests about Japanese textbooks. After a long time, the offensive term was changed back to what it had been before, but the basic system of authorization together with its policy have remained unchanged.

22 Shiroyama Saburō, *War Criminal, the Life and Death of Hirota Kōki*, tr. by John Bester, Kodansha International, 1977.

A Cultural History of Postwar Japan

The Dutch judge Bernard Röling, who took part in the Tokyo Trials, made a speech entitled 'Aspects of the Nuremberg and Tokyo Trials' in the Dutch Academic Council in 1978, in which he reaffirmed his judgment that Hirota was innocent, which he had expressed as a minority opinion at the time of the Trials. He also maintained that 'his policies should not be called criminal in the light of the legal concepts current at the time', and expressed the opinion that he had adopted dangerous policies whose methods were not those of military aggression but of indirect aggression; once these policies were connected with the build-up of armaments, they increased the strength of the military, and in due course enabled the military to wrest the leadership from Hirota. This article appeared in Japanese as 'Hirota Kōki o saishin suru' (Retrial of Hirota Kōki) in *Chūō Kōron*, July 1983. Röling took part in the 'International Symposium on the "Tokyo Trials"' which was held in Tokyo on 28 and 29 May 1983. This symposium made possible, 35 years after the event, a wider perspective on the Tokyo Trials. Ōnuma Yasuaki writes that the Trials 'are related to the responsibility of leadership and to the noteworthy concept of obligatory civil disobedience towards illegal commands by the state', in '"Bunmei no sabaki" "shōsha no sabaki" o koete' (Beyond the 'trials by civilization' and 'trials by the victors'), *Chūō Kōron*, August 1983.

23 Takeda Taijun, *Luminous Moss*, tr. by Shibuya Yasaburō and Sanford Goldstein, in *This Outcast Generation and Luminous Moss*, Tuttle, 1967.

24 Kinoshita Junji, *Between God and Man, a Judgement on War Crimes*, tr. by Eric J. Gangloff, University of Tokyo Press, 1979.

25 Included in the previously mentioned *Testaments of the Century*.

26 *See reference 25.*

27 Inoue Kiyoshi, *Tennō no Sensō Sekinin* (The Emperor's Responsibility in the War), Gendai Hyōronsha, 1975.

Kojima Noboru, in *Tennō* (Emperor), Bungei Shunjūsha, 5 vols., 1974, weaves in episodes such as the Emperor's rejection by his own decision of a peace initiative when the Army General Staff desired peace with China (just before Konoe's statement that he would not deal with Chang Kai Shek's government), but on the whole he presents an image of an upright Emperor trying to be a constitutional monarch.

142

28 Postwar opinion polls on the issue are as follows:

	Maintain Emperor system %	Abolish %
1946	86	11
1948	90	4
1956	82	16
1957 (Feb.)	81	15
1957 (Aug.)	87	11
1965	83	13

NHK Hōsō Yoron Chōsajo (ed.) *Zusetsu Sengo Yoronshi* (Illustrated History of Postwar Public Opinion Polls).

29 Sasaki Gen, 'Orokamono no hi' (The Monument to the Stupid), in Shisō no Kagaku Kenkyūkai (ed.), *Kyōdō Kenkyū - Shūdan* (Joint Research: Groups), Heibonsha, 1976.

3 Comics in Postwar Japan

30 Coulton Waugh, *The Comics*, The Macmillan Co., New York, 1947.

31 George McManus, *Bringing Up Father*, Herb Galewitz (ed.), Bonanza Books, 1973. Looking back through this book at *Bringing Up Father*, one can understand how it was received in Japan as a guide to styles of living after the First World War. One look at this comic must have immediately made clear what a flapper, for example, was. A revolution in sex and marriage, a weakening of parental authority, a challenge to masculine culture through the feminization of culture: all these themes were found in visible form in this comic strip.

32 *Asahi Graph*, January 1925.

33 Niijima Jō, *Hakodate Kikō* (Journey to Hakodate); *Hakodate Dasshutsu no Ki* (Escape from Hakodate); *Hakodate yori no Ryakki* (Brief Note from Hakodate). Unpublished journals.

34 Kishida Ginkō, *Usun Nikki* (Wusung Diary). Unpublished journal.

35 Miyao Shigeo, *Nippon no Giga: Rekishi to Fūzoku* (Japanese Cartoons – their history and social background), Daiichi Hōki Shuppan, 1967. The following books deal in detail with the cartoons in the Hōryūji ceiling: Kuno Takeshi, *Hōryūji kondō tenjōita rakugaki* (Ceiling cartoons on the ceiling of Hōryūji Golden Pavilion), in *Bijutsu Kenkyū*, No. 140, 1947; *Nara Rokudaiji Taikan* (The Six Major Temples of Nara), Vol. I, *Hōryūji* (1), Iwanami Shoten, 1972.

36 *See reference 35.*

37 Yashiro Yukio, *Watashi no Bijutsu Henreki* (My Pilgrimage in Art), Iwanami Shoten, 1972.

A Cultural History of Postwar Japan

38 Ichikawa Hakugen, *Ikkyū*, NHK Bukkusu, Nihon Hōsō Shuppan Kyōkai, 1970.

39 Tominaga Ken'ichi (ed.), *Nippon no Kaisō Kōzō* (The Class Structure of Japan), Tokyo Daigaku Shuppankai, 1979, where he writes: 'One reason for the difficulty in drawing a sketch map to illustrate contemporary Japanese society is that people have practically no concept of "boundary" between the different strata. . . . Even when discussing the question of nearly all Japanese thinking of themselves as middle class, the above-mentioned awareness is vital.' For this reason, Tominaga described Japanese class structure using the multiple variables of occupational status, education, income, assets, life style and power, without combining them into one variable. This means that it is more appropriate in the case of Japan to talk specifically in terms of the position of a graduate of the law faculty of Tokyo University in the Ministry of Finance. Apparently there is a strong sense of belonging to groups such as being an employee of Electric Power Supply, or a player with the Giants Baseball Team, but an awareness of belonging to the working class or the middle class is lacking in Japanese class structure.

40 Because of the great economic growth since 1955, the real spending power of the individual Japanese citizen rose four to five times in the 20 years to 1975. In addition to this is the fact that class divisions are not strong in Japanese culture. Consequently, opinion polls since 1977 have continued to show that fully 90% of people reply that they belong to the middle class. Bureau of Economic Planning, *Kokumin Seikatsu Senkōdo Chōsa* (Surveys of Preferences in National Life), November 1975.

41 Kata Kōji, *Kamishibai Shōwashi* (History of the Picture-card Show in the Showa Period), Ōbunsha, 1979.

42 Kajii Jun, *Sengo no Kashihon Bunka* (The Culture of Postwar Lending Libraries), Tōkōsha, 1976.

43 During the seventies and eighties the number of *manga* titles published in Japan was phenomenal; while publishers of normal books were going bankrupt, those who relied mostly on *manga* could rest easy. The year 1977 was a bad one for ordinary magazines, but boys' and girls' comic magazines significantly increased their sales. In that year, *manga* amounted to 28% of all material published in Japan. In the following year, 1978, boys' *manga* had a growth of over 20%. According to a survey by the Shuppan Kagaku Kenkyūjo (Research Institute for Publication Science), with 4,044 new titles published between January and October 1978, and total sales of 123,460,000, 65% of titles and 70% of total sales were taken by *manga*. *Hyakka Nenkan* (Annual Encyclopaedia Supplement), Heibonsha, 1979. To mention new types of *manga*, not just quantity, Shirato Sanpei, Mizuki Shigeru and Tsuge Yoshiharu all started out with the small circulation comic magazine called *Garo*.

It is a difficult task to make a comprehensive survey of *manga*. In *Sengo Mangashi Nōto* (Jottings of Postwar *Manga* History), Kinokuniya Shinsho, 1975, Ishiko Junzō has recorded names of works, their date of publication and the names of the magazines they appeared in. Soeda

144

References

Yoshiya's *Manga Bunka* (*Manga* Culture), Kinokuniya Shoten, 1983, treats *manga* quantitatively and considers their significance in postwar Japanese society. The first foreign book written about Japanese *manga* is Schodt, Frederik, L., *The Manga! Manga! The World of Japanese Comics*, Kodansha International 1983.

44 Inaba Michio, 'Sore de mo anata wa osuki? – Shōnen mangashi ni miru taikō genshō' (So you still like them? – the retrogressive phenomenon as seen in boys' comic magazines) in the monthly *Sōhyō*, January 1978; Tsumura Takashi, *Mangateki na keikan no joshidaisei koroshi jiken* (The *Manga*-like murder of female college students by a policeman), in *Sōhyō*, March, 1978. This controversy was waged for a year in the pages of *Sōhyō*.

45 *See note 39.*

4 Vaudeville Acts

46 Don Rodrigo de Vivero, *Don Rodrigo's Record of Things Heard and Seen in Japan* (Appendix: *Report on the Exploration of the Biscay Gold and Silver Islands*) Japanese translation by Murakami Naojirō, Ikoku Sōsho, Shūnnansha, 1919; Kawazoe Noboru, *Kon Wajirō no ryūkōron* (Kon Wajirō's fashion theory), in Gendai Fūzoku Kenkyūkai (Research Institute for Contemporary Customs), ed. *Gendai Fūzoku*, No. 3, 1979; see also Kon Wajirō (1888–1973), *Kon Wajirōshū* (A Collection of Kon Wajirō's Works), Vol. 9, Domesu Shuppan 1972.

47 *See reference 46.*

48 E. S. Morse, *Japan Day by Day*, 1–3, 1917, Japanese translation by Ishikawa Kin'ichi, Tōyō Bunko, Heibonsha, 1970. Morse first visited Japan in 1877. His biography was written by Dorothy Wayman: *Edward Sylvester Morse* (2 vols.), 1942. Japanese translation by Ninagawa Chikamasa, Chūō Kōron Bijutsu Shuppan, 1976.

49 B. H. Chamberlain, *Things Japanese* (2 vols.), 1905. Japanese translation by Takanashi Kenkichi, Tōyō Bunko Heibonsha, 1969. Chamberlain was in Japan from 1873 to 1911.

50 Ernest Satow, *Ichi Gaikōkan no Mita Meiji Ishin* (The Meiji Restoration as Seen by a Foreign Diplomat). Japanese translation by Sakata Seiichi, Iwanami Bunko, 1960.

51 Orikuchi Shinobu, *Nihon Bungaku no Hatten* (The Development of Japanese Literature), 1931. Reprinted in *Orikuchi Shinobu Zenshū* (Collected Works of Orikuchi Shinobu), Chūkō Bunko, 1976. Orikuchi's theories about banquet entertainments, or art forms which developed specifically for use at drinking parties, were expounded in several of his writings. They were developed by scholars who were influenced by Orikuchi, and who attempted to verify his theories: Ikeda Yasaburō, *Nihon Geinō Denshōron* (The Transmission of Japanese Performing Arts), Chūō Kōronsha, 1962; Tada Michitarō, *Shigusa no Nihon Bunka* (The Japanese Culture of Gesture), Chikuma Shobō, 1972.

52 Fujiwara no Sadaie (1162–1241) was 38 years old at the time, and had just been granted leave to attend the palace as a court poet.

A Cultural History of Postwar Japan

53 For the history of *manzai*, refer to the following specialist historical research: Morita Yoshinori, *Chūsei Senmin to Zatsugeinō no Kenkyū* (Research in Medieval Outcasts and Miscellaneous Performing Arts), Yūzankaku, 1974; Hayashiya Tatsusaburō, *Chūsei Geinōshi no Kenkyū* (Research into the History of the Medieval Performing Arts), Iwanami Shoten 1960.

54 For a history of *manzai* since the Meiji Period see Yoshida Tamesaburō, *Manzai Taiheiki* (A *Manzai* Chronicle of the Great Peace), Sanwa Tosho, 1964; Yoshida Tamesaburō, *Manzai Fūsetsuroku* (Manzai Weathering the Blizzard), Kyūgei Shuppan, 1978. For a history which comes up to the present day see: Maeda Isamu, *Kamigata Manzai Happyakunenshi* (Eight hundred years of *manzai* in the Kamigata Region), Sugimoto Shoten, 1975; Misumi Haruo, *Sasuraibito no Geinōshi* (History of the Performing Arts of Wayfarers), NHK Bukkusu, Nihon Hōsō Shuppan Kyōkai, 1976.

55 The two wits were Akita Minoru (1905–1977) and Nagaoki Makoto (1904–1976). Nagaoki Makoto, *Kamigata Shōgei Kenbunroku* (Record of my Experiences as a Comedian in the Kamigata Region), Kyūgei Shuppan, 1977; Akita Minoru, *Watakushi wa Manzai Sakusha* (I am a *Manzai* Writer), Bungei Shunjūsha, 1975.

For an appraisal of Akita Minoru, see Yamamoto Akira 'Akita Minoru no warai to wa nan de atta ka' (The Humour of Akita Minoru) in *Kimigata Geinō*, Special Issue on Akita Minoru, April 1978.

56 It is difficult to make adequate records of a popular art like *manzai*, which is always in a state of flux. The earliest treatment is Yanagita Kunio's (1875–1962) *Kebōzukō* (Reflections of a Long-haired Priest), 1914. Taking a hint from this, Hayakawa Kōtarō wrote in 1927 *Sanshū Tokura no Kagura no Saizō no Koto* (On the Saizō in the Kagura of Tokura, Mikawa County). Further, the magazine *Geinō Tōzai* published from 1975 to 1977 'An exchange of letters concerning the Saizō market' by Ozawa Shōichi and Nagai Hiro'o, which investigated the way in which the *tayū-saizō* team was formed.

A book which deals with *manzai* in relation with other popular performing arts is Ei Rokusuke's *Geinintachi no Geinōshi* (History of Performing Arts and Artists), Bunshun Bunko, Bungei Shunjūsha, 1975 (first appeared 1969).

57 Collier, John Payne, *Punch and Judy*, Thomas Hailes, 1823. The importance of the role of Punch seems to have been early realized in Japan among people involved in the puppet theatre, and is commented on by Minamie Jirō (1902–) who was concerned with puppet drama since the Taishō Period. For example: *Kindai Ningyōgeki no Genryū o Saguru – Fuausto to Panchi* (Tracing the Origins of the Modern Puppet Theatre – Faust and Punch), Ikadasha, 1972. This book originally appeared in 1942 during the war, with a preface by Naruse Mukyoku giving an account of his friendship with the author since the Taishō Period.

58 When these lectures were given in the spring of 1980, unknown to me there had already been in Japan a revival of *manzai*. A new style with a

146

new designation, 'The Manzai', presumably signifies an international-ization of *manzai* art. Detailed discussions of the development of this new stream can be found in the following: Inoue Hiroshi, *Manzai – Osaka no Warai* (*Manzai* – the Humour of Osaka) Sekai Shisōsha, 1981; Minami Hiroshi, Nagai Hiro'o, Ozawa Shōichi (eds.), *Irodoru – Iromono no Sekai* (Makeup – the World of Vaudeville), Hakusuisha, 1981; Tsuganezawa Satohiro, *Masumedia no Shakaigaku – Jōhō to Goraku* (The Sociology of the Mass Media – Information and Entertainment), Sekai Shisōsha, 1982.

The plain-speaking narrative style of Biito Takeshi, the new starplayer of Manzai, slashing out at wheedling humanism, is quite different from the style which has been broadcast on the mass media in the 30–odd years since the war, and arguments for and against it enlivened the print media in 1982. By 1983, the television programme which features Biito Takeshi's character Takechan Man, an extraordinary character who disregards realism, had become one of the most popular programmes on television.

5 Legends of Common Culture

59 The generations are divided first by whether or not one is old enough to remember the defeat in 1945 – that is, whether one remembers the war or not; the next big division is whether one accepts television as a normal part of everyday life or not. This is the division between the television generation and the pre-television generation. This is the degree to which television has changed the lives of the Japanese.

One might try to pinpoint this exactly with the date of the first television transmission in 1953, but it was not until 1961 that the number of people watching television surpassed those listening to the radio. In 1962, the number of sets registered as NHK viewers reached 10 million and the average daily viewing time passed the three-hour mark. Kitamura Hideo and Nakano Osamu (eds.), *Nihon no Terebibunka* (Japanese TV Culture), Yūhikaku, 1983.

60 The word *tarento* ('talent', TV personality) was not associated with the beginning of radio in the mid-1920s but entered the Japanese language with the start of television. This is because the methods of television production were learnt from America, and American-English terms came along with the knowhow. According to Fukuda Teiryō, the term *tarento* refers to a person appearing on television who displays a talent for communication, which is fully exploited in the relationship with the mass audience of television. 'The talent of the TV personality is acknowledged as something truly outstanding amongst the talents produced by the masses,' Okamoto Hiroshi and Fukuda Teiryō, *Gendai Tarentorojii* (Contemporary Talentology), Hōsei Daigaku Shuppankyoku, 1966.

The masses entrust a part of their emotions to the TV personality. This is enacted on a daily basis by such dating programmes as *Panchi de deeto* (Dates with Punch), and on a larger scale, like a big festival, by the end-of-year NHK Song Contest.

61 Yanagita Kunio, *Kokyō Nanajūnen* (Seventy Years of my Birth-place), Nojigiku Bunko, 1959.

A Cultural History of Postwar Japan

62 The word 'parody' (*parodii*) was not commonly used in Japan even before the war, and certainly not during it. Not until the 1970s did it become part of everyday Japanese, being used widely in weeklies and in pictorial magazines and comics. This probably means that, because the movement to criticize authority lost the vigour it used to have in the period 1945–1970 and was stifled in the 1970s and 1980s, interest was shown in a mode of expression which tried to hint at something different under the cover of universally accepted sayings. This was also a revival of the popular culture which had existed in the middle Edo Period, when the foreign loan word *parodii* did not exist.

However, even if parody does not incur the harsh sentence of exile to a distant island as in the Edo Period, it does not necessarily get off scot-free. Maddo Amano replaced the skiers in the photograph of a snow-covered mountain by mountain photographer Shirakawa Yoshikazu with big tyres rolling down the slopes. He was sued by Shirakawa in 1970 and brought to trial. At the first hearing he was found guilty, innocent at the second hearing, while the third hearing (at the Supreme Court), on 28 March 1980, ordered a rehearing of the second trial's verdict.

63 A look at the Sunday Great River Dramas of the 1970s shows that of ten works two were dramas about the Meiji Restoration (*Katsu Kaishū* and *Kashin*), and one was on the Chūshingura theme (*Genroku Taiheiki*). Furthermore, three years later in 1982, another Chūshingura drama (*Tōge no Gunzō*) appears.

Title	Period of screening	Popularity rating (%)
Momi no Ki wa Nokotta	Jan.–Dec. 1970	29.9
Haru no Sakamichi	Jan.–Dec. 1971	22.1
Shin Heike Monogatari	Jan.–Dec. 1972	21.4
Kunitori Monogatari	Jan.–Dec. 1973	22.5
Katsu Kaishū	Jan.–Dec. 1974	22.0
Genroku Taiheiki	Jan.–Dec. 1975	24.9
Kumo to Kaze to Niji to	Jan.–Dec. 1976	23.8
Kashin	Jan.–Dec. 1977	17.1
Ōgon no Hibi	Jan.–Dec. 1978	23.8
Kusa Moeru	Jan.–Dec. 1979	19.3

As of 16 July 1983, the morning serialized novel *Oshin* has reached an unprecedented popularity rating of 58.4% (since a rating of 1% represents a million viewers, this represents 58 million viewers throughout the country). Since *Oshin* is the life story of one woman including the period of the Fifteen Years' War, it is in the same dramatic mould as other Great River Drama favourites. In both *Oshin* and *Hatoko no Umi* a deserter from the Japanese Army appears in the supporting role.

148

References

NHK Television's morning serialized novels in the seventies were as follows:

Title	Period of screening	Popularity rating (%)
Niji	April '70 – April '71	15.4
Mayuko Hitori	April '71 – April '72	17.5
Ai yori Aoku	April '72 – March '72	20.2
Kita no Kazoku	April '73 – April '74	18.9
Hatoko no Umi	April '74 – April '75	21.2
Mizuiro no Toki	April '75 – Oct. '75	19.6
Ohayōsan	Oct. '75 – April '76	17.7
Kumo no Jūtan	April '76 – Oct. '76	18.0
Hi no Kuni ni	Oct. '76 – April '77	17.1
Ichibanboshi	April '77 – Oct. '77	16.4
Kazamidori	Oct. '77 – April '78	16.2
Oteichan	April '78 – Oct. '78	16.5
Watashi wa Umi	Oct. '78 – April '79	15.5
Maa Neechan	April '79 – Oct. '79	16.4

64 Shiba Ryōtarō's works, taking as their theme the Meiji Restoration, were presented to the Japanese public in the sixties and seventies serialized in the newspapers, in book and paperback form and as television dramas:

> *Moeyo Ken* (Burn, Sword!)
> *Junshi* (Self-immolation)
> *Saigetsu* (Years and Months)
> *Saka no Ue no Kumo* (Cloud on top of the Hill)
> *Tobu ga gotoku* (As if Flying)
> *Ryōma ga Yuku* (Here Goes Ryōma)
> *Yo ni Sumu Hibi* (Days of my Life)
> *Kashin* (The Gods of the Flower Seeds)
> *Kochō no Yume* (Butterfly Dream)

65 Amano Yūkichi, *Santorii Sendenbu* (Suntory Promotion Section) in *Kōza Komyunikeeshon* (Series on Communication), Vol. 7, Kenkyūsha, 1973.

66 Matsumoto Seichō, *Hansei no Ki* (The Chronicle of Half a Lifetime), Shinchō Bunko, 1970, enlarged ed., Kawade Shobō Shinsha, 1977, first appeared in the magazine *Bungei*, August 1963 to January 1965). Asukai Masamichi, *Matsumoto Seichō no sekai* (The World of Matsumoto Seichō), in *Taishū Bunka no Sōzō* (The Creation of Mass Culture), (*Kōza Komyunikeeshon* [Series on Communication], Vol. 4), Kenkyūsha, 1973.

67 Matsumoto Seichō, *Shōsetsu Teigin Jiken* (The Imperial Bank Incident: a novel), Bungei Shunjūsha, 1959. Morikawa Tetsuro's

149

A Cultural History of Postwar Japan

Gokuchū Ichimannichi (Ten Thousand Days in Gaol), Tosho Shuppansha, 1979, deals with Hirasawa Sadamichi, the man who was suspected of being the criminal and was imprisoned.

68 Tachibana Takashi, *Tanaka Kakuei Kenkyū Zenkiroku* (A Complete Register of Research on Tanaka Kakuei), 2 vols., Kōdansha, 1976.

69 Kim Dae Chung, *Minshū Kyūkoku no Michi* (The Path to Save the Democratic Nation), Shinkyō Shuppansha, 1980. T. K. Sei, *Kankoku kara no Tsūshin* (Letters from South Korea), Iwanami Shinsho, 1974; *Zoku: Kankoku kara no Tsūshin* (More Letters from South Korea), Iwanami Shinsho, 1975. Wada Haruki, *Kankoku kara no Toikake* (Enquiry from South Korea), Shisō no Kagakusha, 1982. Nakazono Eisuke, *Rachi* (Abduction), Kōbunsha, 1983.

70 Sawachi Hisae, *Mitsuyaku – Gaimushō Kimitsu Roei Jiken* (Secret Agreement – the Foreign Affairs Ministry Top Secret Leaks), Chūō Kōronsha, 1974.

6 Trends in Popular Songs since the 1960s

71 Sonobe Saburō, *Nihon Minshū Kayōshikō* (Thoughts on the History of Japanese Popular Song), Asahi Shinbunsha, 1980. The work of Minami Hiroshi and Inui Takashi and others on the analysis of Japanese popular songs is collected in the Shisō no Kagaku Kenkyūkai publication *Yume to Omokage* (Dream and Image), Chūō Kōronsha, 1950. Mita Munesuke analyzes the lyrics and the mood of popular songs up to the era of rapid economic expansion in *Kindai Nihon no Shinjō no Rekishi* (Emotional History of Modern Japan), Kōdansha, 1967. For an analysis of singers and their connection with the mood of the time, including the era of rapid economic growth, see Zakō Jun, *Itsumo Kayōkyoku ga Atta* (There Have Always Been Popular Songs), Shinchōsha, 1983. See also Izawa Sensei Kinen Jigyōkai, *Gakuseki Izawa Shūji Sensei*, Gakusekisha, 1919.

72 Koizumi Fumio and Dan Ikuma, *Ongaku no sekaizu* (World Map of Music) in *Enajii Taiwa*, Esso Petroleum Company Ltd, April 1976.

73 Koizumi Fumio, 'Nihon ongaku no rizumu' (Rhythm in Japanese Music) in *Kokyū suru Minzoku Ongaku* (Vital Ethnomusicology), Seidosha, 1983. First appeared in programme notes for the seventh programme of the National Theatre series *Nihon Ongaku no Nagare* (The Stream of Japanese Music), 1979. See also Koizumi Fumio, 'Kayōkyoku no ongaku kōzō' (The musical structure of popular songs), in Koizumi Fumio *et al.* (eds.), *Uta wa Yo ni tsure* (Song Changes along with the World), Kōdansha, 1978.

74 Satomi Ton, *Uzaemon Densetsu* (The Uzaemon Legend), Mainichi Shinbunsha, 1955; Sawachi Hisae, *Densetsu no naka no purimadonna* (The prima donna in legend) in *Zoku: Shōwashi no Onna* (Sequel to Women in the History of the Shōwa Period), Bungei Shunjūsha, 1983.

75 In the history of Japanese popular song, the speed of the diffusion of 'Katyusha's Song' was amazing. When Tanabe Wakao went on tour after the première of the play *Resurrection*, arriving in Nagasaki at night, he heard young women already singing this song in various places: 'Arriving

ahead of our performance, Katyusha's song was already being sung in this southern province.' Tanabe Wakao, *Haiyū – Butai Seikatsu Gojūnen* (My Life as an Actor – Fifty Years on the Stage), Shunjūsha, 1960.

76 Miyauchi Kanya, *Shichirigahama*, Shinchōsha, 1978. An exile from student life, as a new recruit in the army and connected with a youth institute, Miyauchi composed a melody which merged into the Korean *arian*. See Mihashi Kazuo, *Kinka no Seitaigaku* (Ecology of Forbidden Songs), Ongaku no Tomosha, 1983.

7 Ordinary Citizens and Citizens' Movements

77 Itō Toshio, 'Sākuru zenshi e no kokoromi' (Investigating the history of the 'circle'), in Shisō no Kagaku Kenkyūkai (ed.), *Shūdan* (Groups), Heibonsha, 1976.

78 Wada Yōichi, *Haiiro no Yūmoa* (Grey Humour), Rironsha, 1958. Itō Toshiya, *Maboroshi no 'Stajio Tsūshin' e* (In Pursuit of the Phantom 'Studio Despatch'), Renga Shobō, 1978. This book deals with the history of *Saturday*, based on the memoirs of the small-part actor Saitō Raitarō, and provides a clue to treating this magazine as a citizens' movement. Its viewing of the coffee shop as an arena for the exchange of citizens' opinions also anticipates the postwar citizens' movements of the sixties.

79 *Nakai Masakazu Zenshū* (Collected Works of Nakai Masakazu) (4 vols.), Bijutsu Shuppansha, 1981.

80 During this period, one person who lent strength to the citizens' movement was Hani Gorō (1901–1983). His writings throughout the whole period of the Fifteen Years' War showed a clear trail of civilian protest against militarism: 'Jidō no rekishikan to sono hyōgen' (Children's view of history and its expression), in *Kyōiku* (Education), Iwanami Shoten, May, July and August issues, 1936; *Hakuseki Yukichi* (Arai Hakuseki and Fukuzawa Yukichi), Iwanami Shoten, 1937; *Mikeruangero* (Michelangelo), Iwanami Shinsho, 1939; *Kurooche* (Croce), Kawade Shobō, 1939; 'Meiji Ishin kenkyū' (Research on the Meiji Restoration), in *Chūō Kōron*, January to June issues, 1940; *Bakumatsu ni okeru rinri shisō* (Ethical thought in the Bakumatsu period) in *Kōza – Rinrigaku*, Book 2, Iwanami Shoten, 1940; 'Rekishi oyobi rekishigaku' (History and the study of history), in Kawai Eijirō (ed.), *Gakusei to Rekishi* (Students and History), Nihon Hyōronsha, 1940.

Hani's *Toshi no Ronri* (The Logic of Cities), Keisō Shobō, 1968, is an enlargement of *Toshi* (Cities), Iwanami Shinsho, 1949, and had a great influence on the student movement of the 1960s. It argues for the development of a new political system based on citizens' self-rule, which does not siphon off the citizen's taxes into the national budget of a central government, but allows for a greater portion to be used in regional self-government bodies. For a treatment of Hani's work as a historian during the Fifteen Years' War, see Kitayama Shigeo, *Nihon kindai shigaku no hatten* (The development of the study of history in modern Japan), in *Iwanami Kōza Nihon Rekishi 22 Bekkan 1* (Iwanami History of Japan, No. 22, Appendix 1), Iwanami Shoten, 1963.

81 Tamaki Akira, 'Ajiateki fūdo to nōson' (The Asiatic climate and agricultural villages), in *Keizai Hyōron* (Economic Review), Nihon Hyōronsha, August 1974; *Inasaku Bunka to Nihonjin* (Rice Cultivation and the Japanese), Gendai Hyōronsha, 1977; *Mizu no Shisō* (The Philosophy of Water), Ronsōsha, 1979.

82 *Tanaka Shōzō Zenshū* (Collected Works of Tanaka Shōzō), Iwanami Shoten, 1977–80. After a long period of neglect, Tanaka Shōzō came to attract attention again through the efforts of two people: the research of the philosopher Hayashi Takeji, and, later, technologist and scientist Ui Jun who expounded his significance in the anti-pollution movement and the student-initiated lecture series (Jishukōza), 'Theory of Pollution' (begun 1970).

Hayashi Takeji, 'Teikō no ne' (The Roots of resistance), in *Shisō no Kagaku*, September 1962 issue, commemorating the fiftieth anniversary of the death of Tanaka Shōzō; *Tanaka Shōzō – sono sei to tatakai no 'konpongi'* (The 'basic meaning' of Tanaka Shōzō's Life and Struggle), Nigatsusha, 1974; *Tanaka Shōzō no Shōgai* (The Life of Tanaka Shōzō), Kōdansha, 1976.

Ui Jun, *Kōgai Genron* (Theory of Pollution) 1–3, Supplementary vols. 1–3, Aki Shobō, 1971–4; *Kōgai no Seijigaku – Minamatabyō o otte* (The Politics of Pollution – in pursuit of Minamata Disease), Sanseidō, 1968; *Watakushi no Kōgai Tōsō* (My Pollution Struggle), Ushio Shuppansha, 1971.

Hinata Yasushi, *Tanaka Shōzō Nōto* (Notes on Tanaka Shōzō), Tabata Shoten, 1981; *Hatenaki Tabi* (Endless Journey) (2 vols.), Fukuinkan, 1979.

Tamura Norio, *Kōdoku Nōmin Monogatari* (A Tale of Farmers and Copper Poisoning), Asahi Sensho, 1975. Tamura edits a research magazine, *Tanaka Shōzō to sono Jidai* (Tanaka Shōzō and his age), published by Warashibe Shobō.

Kenneth Strong, *Ox against the Storm*, The University of British Columbia Press, 1977.

83 Taketani Mitsuo (ed.), *Anzensei no Kangaekata* (Attitudes towards Safety), Iwanami Shinsho, 1967. Since then Taketani has contributed towards contemporary criticism with the distinction between special privilege (*tokken*) and human rights (*jinken*), a line of thinking which provides a clue to linking the citizen's life with the work of specialists. 'University professor' is a concept which denotes privilege, whereas 'scholar' is a concept linked with human rights. In this society, our everyday work is carried on by means of privilege; if this does not continually recreate a new direction by an interaction with human rights, privilege will automatically conflict with human rights. See Taketani Mitsuo (ed.) *Tokken to Jinken* (Privilege and Rights), Keisō Shobō, 1979. At the present time (1983) when 90% of Japanese think of themselves as middle class, there are many kinds of links between privilege and the internal life of the citizen which are difficult to control. Because of this difficulty, criticism on behalf of the citizen against science, technology

and, even more broadly, against the academic world in general, which exist as privileged forces severed from human rights, must constantly experiment with new and original ideas.

84 Irokawa Daikichi (ed.), *Minamata no Keiji – Shiranui-kai Sōgō Chōsa Hōkoku* (The Revelation of Minamata – Report of the Joint Inquiry into the Shiranui Sea), Vol. I, Chikuma Shobō, 1983.

On the links between outsiders and the village see the following works by Ishimure Michiko: *Kugai Jōdo*, Kōdansha, 1969; *Ten no Sakana* (The Heavenly Fish), Chikuma Shobō, 1974; *Tsubaki no Umi no Ki* (Chronicle of the Camellia Sea), Asahi Shinbunsha, 1976.

85 Miyaoka Masao, *Sunagawa Tōsō no Kiroku* (Record of the Struggle at Sunagawa), San'ichi Shobō, 1970.

86 Tomura Issaku, *Tatakai ni Ikiru* (Living in Struggle), Aki Shobō, 1970; *No ni Tatsu* (Standing in the Field), San'ichi Shobō, 1974; *Waga Jujika Sanrizuka* (Sanrizuka, My Cross), Kyōbunkan, 1974; *Shosetsu Sanrizuka* (Sanrizuka: a Novel), Aki Shobō, 1975.

For the biography of Ōki Yone, a Sanrizuka farmer, see Makise Kikue, *Kikigaki, Sanrizuka – Dochaku suru Kāsantachi* (The Local-born Mothers of Sanrizuka), Taihei Suppansha, 1973.

Maeda Toshihiko, *Doburoku o Tsukurō* (Let's make home-brewed sake) Nōson Gyoson Bunka Kyōkai, 1981. The home-brewing of sake seen as a form of resistance can be found in Nozoe Kenji and Makabe Hitoshi (eds.), *Doburoku to Teikō* (Home-brewed Sake and Resistance), Taimatsusha, 1976, and further back still in Yanagita Kunio, *Meiji-Taishōshi: Sesōhen* (History of Modern Japan – Signs of the Changing Times), 1930.

87 The magazine *Chiiki Tōsō* (Regional Struggle), Roshinantesha.

88 Nagaoka Hiroyoshi, *Genbaku Minshūshi* (A People's History of the Atomic Bomb), Miraisha, 1977.

89 Shinobu Seizaburō, *Anpo Tōsōshi* (A History of the Security Treaty Struggle), Sekai Shoin, 1961; Hidaka Rokurō (ed.), *Senkyūhyaku Rokujūnen Gogatsu Jūkunichi* (Nineteenth of May, 1960), Iwanami Shinsho, 1960; Koenaki Koe no Kai (ed.), *Mata Demo de Aō* (Let's meet again at the Demonstration), Tokyo Shoten, 1962.

Since these two years of demonstrations, both *Koenaki Koe no Tayori* (News of the Voice for those who have no Voice) and *Ten to Sen* (Dots and Lines), have continued to be active right up to the present.

Kobayashi Tomi, *Kaigara no Machi* (City of Shells), Shisō no Kagakusha, 1980.

90 Betonamu ni Heiwa! Shimin Rengō (ed.), *Shiryō 'Beheiren' Undō* (Documents of Materials on the 'Peace for Vietnam' Committee Movement) (3 vols.), Kawade Shobō Shinsha, 1974; *Beheiren Nyūsu Shukusatsuban* (Pocket Edition 'Peace for Vietnam' Committee News), Beheiren, 1974; *Nandemo Mite Yarō* (We'll look at everything), by Beheiren spokesman Oda Makoto, Kawade Shobō, 1961, shows clearly the wide support enjoyed by this movement.

91 An early critical appraisal of 'Sazaesan' was Imamura Taihei's

Amerika Manga to Nihon Manga – Sazaesan to Burondii (American comics and Japanese comics – Sazaesan and Blondie), in *Shisō no Kagaku*, April 1951 and February 1953.

The wide popularity of *Sazaesan* among Japanese urban dwellers in the 1960s was discussed in *Roku Daitoshi to Shimin* (Six Large Cities and their Citizens), published by the Council of Chief Commissioners of the Planning Enquiry of Specific Cities, Kyoto Town Planning Office, in 1966.

92 Kuno Osamu, 'Heiwa no ronri to sensō no ronri' (The logic of peace and the logic of war), in *Sekai*, November 1949.

93 I am indebted to Taketani Mitsuo for pointing out this distinction to me soon after the war.

8 Comments on Patterns of Life

94 Some idea of how unusual Yanagita was can be gained from reading what he wrote in a magazine article written towards the end of the war when all was dyed in the single colour of nationalism:

> The sad thing about conservatism is that it can only learn from the recent past. For example, the idea of the Preservation of the National Essence in the beginning of the Meiji Period. One can only return to something very soon after the event; therefore old in this sense would only be about as far back as the Tenpō Era (1830–1843). Conservatism then would have meant something like wearing a *tōzan haori* jacket.
>
> This is what conservatism tends to mean. It can probably be seen as a reaction. . . . Any really conscientious scholar will recognize that the times are always changing. The Meiji Period had its own way of life; the Taishō Period had its own way of life. This may include frivolous, or even unnecessary reform, or improvements which are made only in imitation of other people. By and large, each age makes its own different demands. Therefore, while there is sometimes a return to the past, one must recognize that we are going in a different direction. That is the most important thing. (Yanagita Kunio, 'Minkan denshō ni tsuite' (On folklore), in *Bungei Shunjū*, September 1943.)

95 Many hitherto secret documents relating to the Occupation are now being released to the public in America. There are no doubt many things which should be added to the text of this book.

Sodei Rinjirō, *Makkasa no Nisennichi* (MacArthur's Two Thousand Days), Chūō Kōronsha, 1974; Sodei Rinjirō and Fukushima Chūrō (eds.), *Makkasa* (MacArthur), Nihon Hōsō Shuppan Kyōkai, 1983; the letters of Japanese civilians to MacArthur which are now being printed in *Shisō no Kagaku*, August 1983 onwards. The difference between Japanese and American tastes in personal style is clearly seen in the fact that MacArthur, who was the emotional mainstay of the Japanese, was not popular with Americans in the same period. The Japanese found it difficult to understand how MacArthur failed to gain endorsement as a candidate in the presidential election.

96 Shisō no Kagaku Kenkyūkai (centring on Tsukuda Jitsuo) (ed.) *Nihon Senryō* (The Occupation of Japan), Tokuma Shoten, 1972; *Nihon Senryōgun – sono Hikari to Kage* (Light and Dark Sides of the Japanese Occupation Army), 2 vols., Tokuma Shoten, 1978; Takemae Eiji, Amakawa Akira, Hata Ikuhiko, Sodei Rinjirō, *Nihon Senryō Hishi* (The Secret History of the Japanese Occupation), 2 vols., Asahi Shinbunsha, 1977; Kojima Noboru, *Nihon Senryō* (The Occupation of Japan), 3 vols., Bungei Shunjūsha, 1978.

Books based on newly released materials: Takemae Eiji, *Senryō Sengoshi* (Occupation Postwar History), Sōshisha, available through Keisō Shobō, 1980; Morita Yoshiyuki, *Tainichi Senryō Seisaku no Keisei* (The Formation of the Occupation Policy towards Japan), Ashi Shobō, 1982.

For a testimony from within the Occupation army there is Thomas A. Bisson's *Bisson's Memoirs of the Occupation of Japan*, translated into Japanese as *Bisson Nihon Senryō Kaisōki*, by Nakamura Masanori and Miura Yōichi, Sanseidō, 1983.

I myself would pick out Robert King Hall's *Education for a New Japan*, Yale University Press, 1949, as the record most clearly showing the aspirations of a young officer in the Occupation authorities. Now that a considerable time has elapsed since the Occupation, the people involved tend to underplay the idealism of the Americans at the time who feared nothing; this book, published during the Occupation, gives a good picture of the atmosphere of the Occupation army at the time, and an aspect which we are apt to lose sight of is in fact well represented.

97 See the reference to Tominaga Ken'ichi (ed.), *The Class Structure of Japan*, in reference 39, above.

98 A Ministry for Agriculture publication, *Shokuryō Jukyūhyō* (Table of Supply and Demand of Foodstuffs) gives the following rates of self-sufficiency in grain (these figures assume that supply and demand of rice have levelled out since 1966):

Year	%
1955	87
1956	79
1957	81
1958	80
1959	83
1960	82
1961	75
1962	73
1963	63
1964	63
1965	62

1966	58
1967	56
1968	54
1969	49
1970	45
1971	46
1972	42
1973	40
1974	39
1975	40
1976	37
1977	35
1978	34
1979	33
1980	33
1981	33
1982	33

If we look only at the staple food grains from among these,

Year	%
1960	89
1961	83
1962	84
1963	76
1964	79
1965	80
1966	80
1967	79
1968	79
1969	76
1970	74
1971	73
1972	71
1973	70
1974	69
1975	69
1976	68
1977	67
1978	68
1979	69
1980	69
1981	69
1982	69

According to the Secretary of the Survey Department in the Ministry for Agriculture, the definition of self-sufficiency in food is as follows:

$$\text{Food self-sufficiency} = \frac{\text{Amount of national production}}{\text{Amount of national consumption}}$$

National consumption = production + imports − exports − variations in stockpiles.

'Grain' means rice, barley, wheat, rye, miscellaneous grains (corn, buckwheat and so on), and does not include lentils (beans) and potatoes.

It should be noted that since 1980, owing to enforced regulation of production and to irregularities of weather, self-sufficiency in rice has dropped to below 100%.

The generation of Japanese who grew up in the period of rapid economic growth and the generation who grew up before, during and immediately after the war had such different food, were so different in height, that physically they might almost be called a different race of people. Taking the age of 20 as the cut-off point, the Ministry of Social Welfare published the following table of average heights (measured in centimetres), starting ten years after the beginning of rapid economic growth:

	Age 20 years	
Year	*Men*	*Women*
1965	164.9	153.8
1975	166.9	156.1
1979	169.7	156.9

If we select those between 30 and 39 years, the figures are as follows:

	Age 30–39 years	
Year	*Men*	*Women*
1965	162.7	151.1
1975	163.8	152.7
1979	166.0	153.4

In 1965, at the age of 43, I was 162 cm in height, which probably made me slightly shorter than the average 43-year-old Japanese at the time. (I was extremely short among city dwellers.) Now at this height, when I put myself against 20-year-olds whose average height is over 170 cm, I feel they are outlandishly big. Add to this the differences in body language which come from the cultural changes, one realizes that a totally different culture has been born in Japan since the 1960s.

Nevertheless, putting aside such bodily changes and the world of physical gesture, we cannot say that the Japanese people are losing their Japanese culture on the level of thought. In fact there has been a tendency since the 1960s among the younger generation towards conservatism of thought, and according to Hayashi Chikio, basing arguments on the surveys of national spirit by the Research Institute of Statistics, they demonstrate an ethos which respects tradition. He argues that in younger groups the modern and tradition are not in conflict. Hayashi Chikio, *Nihonjin Kenkyū Sanjūnen* (Thirty Years of Research into the Japanese), Shiseidō, 1981.

99 Society for the Study of Contemporary Customs (ed.), *Gendai Fūzoku* (Contemporary Customs), No. 3, 1979. This research society strives to define 'contemporary customs' in their differences from pre-contemporary customs, based on the sense of the contemporary as defined by Kuwahara Takeo, 'Gendai Nihon Bunmei ni tsuite' (On contemporary Japanese civilization) in *Bunmei Kansōshū* (Collection of Reflections on Civilization), Chikuma Shobō 1975:

> Next, I would like to point out that by 'contemporary' I mean by
> and large the 1960s and onwards. . . . I would include the frustration
> of the Ampo demonstrations, but mainly I believe that rapid
> economic growth and the concomitant radical social changes
> became evident in the 1960s and after.

100 According to the Prime Minister's Office's *Kokumin Seikatsu ni Kansuru Yoron Chōsa* (Public Opinion Polls relating to National Life), the proportion of people regarding themselves as middle class has not changed greatly from the 1960s to the early 1980s. In the same period, those replying that their circumstances are upper class ranged from 0.6% to 0.7%, and lower class as shown in the table. Since it is based on subjective assessment the survey cannot be said to represent actual conditions, but even with making such allowances, it cannot be denied that in this period a middle-class consciousness was widespread.

The meaning which can be placed on these poll results was debated by Murakami Yasusuke, Kishimoto Shigenobu, Tominaga Ken'ichi, Takabatake Michitoshi, and Mita Munesuke in the *Asahi Shinbun*, 20 May to 24 August 1977.

According to the investigation of Tominaga *et al.* ten years after the defeat in 1955, 42% of Japanese assessed themselves as between 'upper middle' and 'lower middle', and by 1975 this had become 76%. All participants of the debate agreed on this. However, Kishimoto said that even in the sixties and seventies people who represented the 'power of the organisation' in the corporate world were still exceptional in that they were merely large individual shareholders, or the highest management executives, and that homogenization of income did not signify the establishment of a homogeneous new middle-class stratum. Tominaga saw the increase of 'status inconsistency', compared with before the 1960s, as an important change. People with high income are not necessarily those with the highest prestige; people with high prestige and status are not necessarily those in the highest positions of power. Thus, there are large discrepancies between multiple constituent factors of class status.

Year	See themselves as middle class %	See themselves as lower class %
1965	86	8
1966	87	7
1967	89	7
1968	86	8
1969	89	8
1970	89	7
1971	90	6
1972	89	7
1973	90	6
1974 (Jan.)	91	6
(Nov.)	90	5
1975 (May)	90	5
(Nov.)	90	5
1976 (May)	90	6
(Nov.)	90	5
1977	90	5
1978	89	6
1979	91	5
1980	89	7
1981	88	7
1982	89	7
1983	89	7

It should be noted that while there is a high degree of correlation between education and occupational status (0.42), the correlation between education and income is only 0.38.

The significance of the concept of the middle class for postwar Japanese culture was early pointed out by Katō Hidetoshi, *Chūkan Bunka* (Middle-class Culture), Heibonsha, 1957, which in retrospect was a highly prophetic book. For a book which explains what kind of pitfalls were faced in this period by the Japanese masses (or rather, to put it my way, the Japanese as a mass,) as 'people who abandoned scepticism towards industrialism and democracy', see Nishibe Susumu, *Taishū e no Hangyaku* (Treason against the Masses), Bungei Shunjūsha, 1983.

101 The Tokyo Metropolitan Council survey of workers' household budgets shows that after peaking in July–August 1948, the Engel coefficient decreases; in 1949, it is 10% less than in 1946 and 1947. In January 1948, monthly wages averaged Yen 5,205, actual expenditure was Yen 7,084, of which food was Yen 4,220, giving an Engel's coefficient of

159

59.5%. In January 1949, monthly wages averaged Yen 11,194, actual expenditure Yen 14,046, of which food was Yen 7,987, giving an Engel's coefficient of 56.8% (*Asahi Nenkan*, 1950). On changes since that time, 'Household Income and Expenditure of City Dwellers in all Japan' in Hitotsubashi University Economic Research Institute (ed.), *Kaisetsu: Nihon Keizai Tōkei* (Japanese Econometrics Interpreted), Iwanami Shoten, 1961, gives the following Engel's coefficients:

Year	%
1951	51.6
1952	48.3
1953	45.0
1954	45.5
1955	44.5
1956	43.0
1957	42.0
1958	41.2

It is relevant to mention here increased life expectancy and the ageing of Japanese society. Average life expectancy in Japan in 1980, according to *Kōseishō Tōkei Yōkan* (Statistical Survey of the Ministry of Health), was, for men, 73.32 years, for women 78.83 years. This surpassed the United States, and was about equal with northern European countries (Kōsaka Masataka (ed.), *Sūji de miru Sekai no Ayumi – 1982* (The Development of the World seen in Statistics – 1982), PHP Research Institute, 1982). In 1983 the *Guinness Book of Records* listed Izumi Shigechiyo, a Japanese man (aged 118) as the oldest living person. The proportion of the population over the age of 65 has risen from 4.8% in 1930 to 9% in 1980, and is likely to go on increasing.

102 Aratani Makoto, *Kieta Mizuumi Hachirōgata – Kantakumae no Mizuumi de no Shōnen no Hi no Rōdō* (The Lake that Disappeared – a Boy's Working Day before the Reclaiming of Lake Hachirōgata), Mumei no Nihonjin Sōsho Bessōbon 2, Yamanami Shuppan no Kai, 1977.

103 Iinuma Jirō, 'Hachirōgata to Sanrizuka' (Hachirōgata and Sanrizuka) in *Kyoto Daigaku Gakusei Shinbun*, 1 June 1979.

104 Nomura Masakazu, in *Shigusa no Sekai – Shintai Hyōgen no Minzokugaku* (The World of Gesture – the Ethnology of Body Language), NHK Bukkusu, Nohon Hōsō Shuppan Kyōkai, 1983, says that in Japan toleration of a degree of nakedness in everyday life, a legacy of the southern islands, continued in places right through till the 1960s.

105 Nakano Osamu, 'Kapuseru ningen to katarogu bunka' (Capsule man and catalogue culture), in *Narushisu no Genzai* (Narcissus Today), Jiji Tsūshinsha, January 1983. The typology of 'capsule man' comes from Nakano, *Kopii Taiken no Bunka* (The culture which has experienced copying), Jiji Tsūshinsha, 1975.

106 Gendai Fūzoku Kenkyūkai (ed.), *Gendai Fūzoku* (Contemporary Customs), No. 2, 1978.

107 According to Ienaga Saburō, in *Zōhō Kaitei: Nihonjin no Yōfukukan no Hensen* (Changes in Japanese Attitudes to Western Dress: expanded and enlarged ed.), Domesu Shuppan, 1982 (1st ed., 1976), for primary school students in central Tokyo, Western dress came to predominate over Japanese dress between 1922 and 1926.

Yamamoto Akira (ed.) *Shōwa no Kyōkō* (Shōwa Panic), third volume of *Zusetsu: Shōwa no Rekishi* (Illustrated History of the Shōwa Period), Shūeisha, 1979, treats the change towards Western clothes in both men and women in various places. It was towards the end of the Taishō Period (that is, the early 1920s) that Western clothes took precedence among urban men in the workplace. A survey by Kon Wajirō in the streets of Ginza and Nihonbashi on a public holiday in 1937 showed that only 25% of women were in Western dress. Women's dress did not become predominantly Western throughout the country until after the war.

108 The results of this film were later collated as a survey report. See Shōhin Kagaku Kenkyūjo and CDI (eds.), *Seikatsuzai Seitaigaku – Gendai Katei no Mono to Hito* (Ecology of Livelihood Assets – Things and People in the Contemporary Family), 2 vols., Riburoripōto, 1980–3.

109
Hoshino Yoshirō, *Kōkishin to kyūhakukan no akekure* (Absorption in curiosity and a sense of urgency), in Tsurumi and Hoshino, *Nihonjin no Ikikata* (How the Japanese Live), Kōdansha, 1966:

The boldness with which the Japanese jump at new foreign goods
and technologies is in strong contrast with European industry. What
is more, Japanese industry often does not accurately calculate the
practical value of the importation. The introduction of foreign
technology has greater economic influence than just on an
individual, with the result that a whole industry often causes a stir
by falling into ruin.

However, on the other hand, characteristic Japanese attitudes
and capabilities are eloquent. Japanese technologists tinker
indefatigably with foreign technologies which were never meant for
Japanese conditions; by making carefully thought-out
improvements, they produce an exquisite balance, and make them
into something Japanese which finally realize great profits for the
industry.

Hoshino here draws attention to the social psychology whereby the excitement of the discovery of new foreign technologies spreads like wildfire because of a common curiosity among engineers of the same generation.

110 The rate of increase in the postwar Japanese population fell in 1957 to single figures per thousand and has not increased significantly since then up to the present:

Year	Total population (in 000's)	Rate of population increase (no. per thousand people)
1946	75,750	49.94
1947	78,101	31.05
1948	80,002	24.34
1949	81,773	22.13
1950	83,200	17.45
1951	84,541	16.13
1952	85,808	14.95
1953	86,981	13.67
1954	88,239	12.15
1955	89,276	11.75
1956	90,127	10.04
1957	90,928	8.39
1958	91,767	9.23
1959	92,641	9.53
1960	93,419	8.39
1961	94,287	9.29
1962	95,181	9.48
1963	96,156	10.25
1964	97,182	10.67
1965	98,275	11.25
1966	99,036	7.74
1967	100,196	11.71
1968	101,331	11.33
1969	102,536	11.89
1970	103,720	11.55
1971	105,145	13.71
1972	107,595	14.09
1973	109,104	14.02
1974	110,573	13.46
1975	111,940	12.36
1976	113,089	10.26
1977	114,154	9.42
1978	115,174	8.94
1979	116,133	8.33
1980	117,057	7.96
1981	117,660	5.15

Source: Prime Minister's Office Statistics Department, *Jinkō Suikei* (Population Estimates) and *Kokusei Chōsa* (Survey of the State of the Nation), in Kōsaka Masataka (ed.) *Sūii de miru Nihon no Ayumi – 1982* (Japan's Progress as seen in Figures – 1982), PHP Research Institute, 1982.

111 In this period there was no government regulations aimed at

References

limiting births as in the case for example of China over the same period; it was a voluntary population restraint on the part of the Japanese citizens.

112 Morishima Michio, 'Shin "Shin gunbi keikakuron"' (New 'New armaments planning') and Seki Yoshihiko, 'Hibusō de heiwa wa mamorenai' (Peace cannot be kept without arms), in *Bungei Shunjū*, July 1979; Morishima Michio, 'Shin "Shin gunbi keikakuron" horon' (Supplement to New 'New armaments planning') and Seki Yoshihiko, 'Hibusō de heiwa wa mamorenai horon' (Supplement to Peace cannot be kept without arms), in *Bungei Shunjū*, October 1979.

9 A Comment on Guidebooks on Japan
113 Fay Adams, Walker Brown, Gordon W. Leckie, R. W. W. Robertson, Lester B. Rogers, Carl S. Simonson, *The Story of Modern Nations*, Henry Holt and Co., New York, 1958. For an extensive collection of images of Japan presented in foreign textbooks, see Kokusai Kyōiku Jōhō Sentā, *Kaigai no Kyōkasho ni miru Ikoku Nippon Gurafiti* (Exotic Nippon Graffiti seen in Foreign Textbooks), Jatekku Shuppan, 1983.

114 Richard Tames, *The Japan Handbook*, Paul Norbury Publications, Kent, England, 1978. For a treatment of the not necessarily rosy conditions of Japanese workers, see Satoshi Kamata, *Japan in the Passing Lane*, Pantheon, 1983, with a foreword by Ronald P. Dore. The Japanese version, *Jidōsha Zetsubō Kōjō* (Automobile Despair Factory), was first published by Gendaishi Shuppankai in 1973. Ronald Dore's foreword to the English edition was published in Japanese in *Keizai Hyōron*, Nihon Hyoronsha, October and November issues, 1983.

115 Usami, Mitsuaki and Cheung Hon Chung, *Tokyo*, Chartwell Books, New Jersey, 1978.

116 Ayukawa Nobuo and Yoshimoto Takaaki, *Bungaku no Sengo* (The Postwar Period in Literature), Kōdansha, 1979.

117 Katō Shūichi *et al.*, *Tenkeiki, Hachijūnendai e* (The Age of Transformation – Towards the Eighties), Ushio Shuppansha, 1979.

118 Kyokutei (Takizawa) Bakin (ed.), revised by Rantei Seiran, *Zōho Haikai Saijiki* (The Book of Seasons for Haikai Poets: enlarged edit.) (2 vols.), Seikatsu no Koten Sōsho, Nos. 9 and 10, Yasaka Shobō, 1973. First appeared in November 1851.

119 In the realm of popular culture, there are the essays of Uekusa Jin'ichi, and the parodies and novels of Inoue Hisashi. In the portraits of Yamafuji Shoji, there is a self-conscious effort to recapture the culture of the Edo Period. The 1983 NHK Great River Drama presented an idealized picture of the Edo Period, strategically planned by Tokugawa Ieyasu, in contrast to the civil wars of the fifteenth and sixteenth centuries, and in contrast also to the overseas aggression of Toyotomi Hideyoshi.

120 The literature written in Japanese by Korean residents of Japan is not strictly Japanese literature, but it is an important section of literature written in the Japanese language, and to ignore it one cannot satisfactorily relate the story of Japanese literature, especially in the postwar period.

121 Edwin O. Reischauer wrote in *The Japanese*, Harvard University

163

A Cultural History of Postwar Japan

Press, 1977, that Japan differed from the United States in that there were virtually no underprivileged ethnic and regional groupings, but followed with the statement that there were, however, the problems of the unliberated *burakumin* (descendants of a class of outcastes) and of Koreans resident in Japan. In the Japanese version of this book – Kunihiro Masao (trans.), Bungei Shunjūsha, 1979 – this line is omitted.

This fact reveals a situation where, even more than the Americans, the Japanese are made not to see the discrimination against *burakumin*.

A book by Marie-Josée Balbeau, edited by Morooka Sukeyuki, *Shiritagaranai Nihonjin: Furansujin no mita Burakumondai* (The Japanese Who Turn a Blind Eye: the Buraku Problem as seen by a Frenchwoman), Kashiwa Shobō, 1983, analyses accurately the reaction of the Japanese who are who are coming into contact with Westerners.

122 Nagata Hidejirō, 'Nettai kidai no kangaekata' (How to consider seasonal themes [in *haiku* poetry] in the tropics), in *Nagata Seifū Kushū* (A Collection of the *Haiku* of Nagata Hidejirō), 1958. Quoted in Kamishima Jirō, 'Nihongata hoshushugi – Nagata Hidejirō o tegakari to shite' (Nagata Hidejirō as a clue to the Japanese mould of conservatism), in *Rikkyō Hōgaku*, No. 6, 1964.

123 Tsukuda Jitsuo, *Senryō no Sekaishi* (A World History of Occupation) in Shisō no Kagaku Kenkyūkai (ed.), *Nihon Senryōgun – sono Hikari to Kage* (The light and shadow of the Japanese Occupation Army), Vol. 1, Tokuma Shoten, 1978.

In 1918 the problem arose of the god to be enshrined in a Shinto shrine in Korea. The Korean Governor's headquarters had began preparations on the basis of the decision to enshrine the two mainstays, Amaterasu Ōmikami and the Emperor Meiji, but Imaizumi Sadasuke, Ashizu Kōjirō, Kamo Momoki, and Hida Kageki among others argued strongly that 'the god to be enshrined in the Korean shrine should naturally be a god with a close connection with the land of Korea; that is, the god who was responsible for the creation of Korea should be venerated'. Ashizu in particular had been thinking along these lines ever since the annexation of Korea, and had explained his position to the first Superintendant-General of Korea, Itō Hirobumi, when he visited Shimonoseki on his way to take up his new post. Ashizu's August 1925 article, 'Chōsen Jingū ni Kansuru Ikensho' (A statement of personal views on the Korean Shrine), which is included in Jinja Shinpōsha Seikyō Kenkyūshitsu (ed.), *Kindai Jinja Shintōshi* (A Modern History of Shinto and Shinto Shrines), Jinja Shinpōsha, 1976, is also quoted by Tsukuda in his book, cited above.

124 The International House of Japan Library, *Modern Japanese Literature in Translation*, Kodansha International, 1979. According to this Ibuse Masuji's works have been translated into English, German, French, Russian, Korean, Portugese, Thai and Polish. Nakano Shigeharu has been translated into Russian, German, Korean, French, Chinese and English. See *Three Works by Nakano Shigeharu*, translated by Brett de Barry, Cornell University East Asia Papers, No. 21, 1979.

Index

Alphabetical order is word-by-word. Page numbers in **bold** refer to illustrations. Titles of works have been indexed from the text only, authors from both text and references.   MCG

For Product Safety Concerns and Information please contact our EU
representative GPSR@taylorandfrancis.com
Taylor & Francis Verlag GmbH, Kaufingerstraße 24, 80331 München, Germany

www.ingramcontent.com/pod-product-compliance
Lightning Source LLC
Chambersburg PA
CBHW050513280326
41932CB00014B/2305